Contents

THE MEDITERRANEAN
REFRESH COOKBOOK 2022

Over 200 Easy & Delicious Recipes for Everyone

Plus 30Days Meal Plan

Katie Jean

Copyright

Fish and Seafood Recipes 249

Introduction

Because of its wealth of savory components such as fruits, vegetables, whole grains, and heart-healthy fats, the Mediterranean diet is both delicious and healthful. It's also related to a host of health advantages, including brain function support, heart health promotion, and more. Among other things, blood sugar levels are regulated.

Although there are no hard and fast rules for adhering to the Mediterranean diet, there are a few general guidelines to follow the recommendations for incorporating the principles of the diet into your daily routine

The Mediterranean diet is discussed in depth in this book including what it is, how to follow it, and how it might benefit you.

I wish you a lifestyle full of health and wealth.

The Fundamental of Mediterranean Diet

What is Mediterranean Diet

The Mediterranean diet is inspired by the traditional food of Mediterranean countries such as France, Spain, Greece, and Italy.

Although no specific dietary recommendations exist, fruits, vegetables, whole grains, legumes, nuts, seeds, and heart-healthy fats are often recommended. Added sugar, refined cereals, and processed meals should all be avoided.

The Mediterranean diet, according to a growing body of data, may help individuals lose weight and avoid heart attacks, strokes, type 2 diabetes, and early mortality.

As a remedy, those who desire to improve their health and protect themselves against chronic illness are usually advised to follow the Mediterranean diet.

According to dietary recommendations, people should eat the following foods: a diverse selection of fruits, vegetables, and whole grains. Healthy fats may also be found in nuts, seeds, and olive oil. moderate dairy and seafood consumption, a tiny bit of white meat, a small amount of red meat, a few eggs, and a small amount of red wine, but only in moderation

A classic Mediterranean diet includes antioxidant-rich fruits, vegetables, whole grains, beans, legumes, nuts, seeds, olive oil, herbs, and spices. It also recommends eating omega-3-rich fish and shellfish on a weekly basis, as well as chicken, eggs, cheese, and yoghurt. The diet forbids the consumption of red meat, sweets, and other processed foods. Red wine is advised in moderation, but it is not essential. Coffee and tea are allowed, but be sure you stay hydrated.

How does Mediterranean diet work?

Specific products may be proven to be more significant in the future as more research on the health advantages of this sort of diet are undertaken. For the time being, however, it seems that rather than particular "superfoods," it is the overall diet approach and range of foods that make this such a healthy way of eating.

This makes sense since if you're eating an unhealthy diet consisting of processed foods, adding one element like olive oil as your lone modification is unlikely to make a major difference in your health. You may be able to lose weight if you adjust your overall diet to include a little less meat and a little more fish, pick healthy fats, and eat more fruits and vegetables.

3

Health benefit of Mediterranean Diet

1. It helps to keep the heart healthy.

The ability of the Mediterranean diet to improve heart health has been extensively studied. The Mediterranean diet has been associated to a lower risk of heart disease and stroke in studies.

When the Mediterranean diet was compared against a low-fat diet, researchers discovered that the Mediterranean diet was more effective at reducing plaque build-up in the arteries, which is a major risk factor for heart disease.

Other studies have shown that the Mediterranean diet may help reduce diastolic and systolic blood pressure, which is beneficial to heart health.

2. It aids in the maintenance of a normal blood sugar level.

The Mediterranean diet emphasizes fruits, vegetables, nuts, seeds, whole grains, and heart-healthy fats.

As a consequence, sticking to this dietary pattern may help to keep blood sugar levels stable and avoid type 2 diabetes.

A Mediterranean diet has been shown in several trials to reduce fasting blood sugar levels and improve haemoglobin A1C levels, a test used to determine long-term blood sugar management.

The Mediterranean diet has also been related to insulin resistance, a condition in which the body's ability to utilize insulin to effectively regulate blood sugar levels is reduced.

3. It aids in the proper functioning of the brain.

According to many studies, the Mediterranean diet is excellent for your brain and may even help you avoid cognitive decline as you age.

In a study including 512 people, following the Mediterranean diet was associated to enhanced memory and decreased levels of multiple risk factors for Alzheimer's disease.

Other studies have connected the Mediterranean diet to a decreased risk of dementia, cognitive impairment, and Alzheimer's disease.

Furthermore, following a Mediterranean diet increased cognitive function, memory, attention, and processing speed in healthy older people, according to a big study.

4. It can help with type 2 diabetes prevention and treatment.

It may seem counterintuitive that a diet consisting in carbohydrate-rich foods like pasta and ancient grains might help with type 2 diabetes management and prevention. There are, however, a few key factors that make this reasonable: The Mediterranean diet emphasizes whole grains and carbohydrates from vegetables, which do not affect blood sugar as much as processed carbs.

A lot of protein and healthy fats are also included in the diet. On the diet, too many sweets and desserts are prohibited.

The Mediterranean lifestyle encourages exercise, which helps with diabetes therapy. A 2014 review of nine distinct studies looked at the influence of the Mediterranean diet on diabetes risk, and the researchers concluded that adopting a Mediterranean diet may cut the risk of diabetes by up to 19 percent.

According to a research published in 2020, stronger adherence to the Mediterranean diet is connected to a decreased incidence of type 2 diabetes.

5. It has the potential to protect you against cancer to some extent.

The Mediterranean diet is well-known for protecting against chronic illnesses including diabetes, heart disease, and metabolic syndrome. This anti-inflammatory and antioxidant-rich diet, it turns out, may also protect against cancer.

According to a 2017 review of research, a Mediterranean diet helps prevent breast cancer, stomach cancer, liver cancer, prostate cancer, and head and neck cancer.

According to the authors, the preventative advantage is "mainly driven by bigger diets of fruits, vegetables, and whole grains."

In 2015, another research evaluated the benefits of a Mediterranean diet to a low-fat diet on breast cancer prevention in women. What were the results?

It's been shown that a Mediterranean diet, especially one supplemented with extra virgin olive oil, may help women fight breast cancer.

6. It has the ability to lower blood pressure and LDL cholesterol.

LDL cholesterol (often known as "bad" cholesterol) and blood pressure are two important markers of health and sickness risk. When either marker is excessively high, it might indicate or cause a health concern.

The Mediterranean diet, for example, is one of several approaches for regulating and decreasing blood pressure and LDL cholesterol. In 2014, scientists studied the diets of over 800 firefighters to examine how their eating habits affected important health indicators, and they found that the more closely the men followed a Mediterranean diet, the better their cholesterol levels were. In a 2018 study, researchers discovered that the Mediterranean diet may reduce blood pressure in those with and without hypertension in general, while the authors noted that more research is required to completely understand the Mediterranean diet's effects on blood pressure.

7. It promotes weight loss, which is helpful.

Fiber is abundant in Mediterranean diets, which benefits with weight loss. Fiber-rich meals keep you satisfied for longer, which helps you lose weight and speed up your metabolism. Replace carbohydrate foods with high-fiber fruits, vegetables, and nuts for the best results. The Mediterranean diet, with its focus on genuine, whole foods, particularly those rich in fiber, is a good option for anybody looking to enhance their metabolic health. Gandhi notes, "A high-fiber diet helps with diabetes and glucose intolerance, keeps you full, and prevents you from gaining weight."

Indeed, the Mediterranean diet has been linked to a decreased risk of chronic illnesses such as type 2 diabetes and metabolic syndrome, as well as being more effective for weight reduction than a low-fat diet.

8. **It improves the health of the intestines**.

Because of the high consumption of whole grains, fruits, and vegetables, this diet is strong in fiber, vitamins, minerals, and antioxidants, all of which may help gut health by feeding the helpful probiotic bacteria that live there and lowering inflammation. According to one research, primates given a plant-heavy Mediterranean diet had a much larger population of good gut flora than those fed a traditional meat-heavy Western diet. Gut health is connected to mental health, which may explain why a Mediterranean diet is associated with a more positive mood.

9. **It aids in the improvement of sleep quality**.

In a 2018 study Trusted Source, researchers looked examined how the Mediterranean diet impacts sleep. According to their results, elderly people who eat a Mediterranean diet sleep better. Diet did not seem to have an effect on sleep quality in younger people.

Which Food Are Allowed

It's controversial whether foods belong in the Mediterranean diet, partly because of regional disparities. The majority of research focused on a diet rich in nutrient-dense plant foods and low in animal products and meat. However, it is advised that you consume fish and seafood at least twice a week.

Regular physical exercise, communal meals, and stress reduction are all part of the Mediterranean way of life. Fruits and vegetables may be used fresh, frozen, dried, or canned, but check package labels for added sugar and salt. The following healthy Mediterranean foods should be included in your diet: Tomatoes, broccoli, kale, spinach, onions, cauliflower, carrots, Brussels sprouts, cucumbers, potatoes, sweet potatoes, turnips, turnips, turnips, turnips, turnips, turnips, turnips, turnips, turnips, turnips, turnips, turnips, turnips, turnips, turnips, turnips Apples, bananas, oranges, pears, strawberries, grapes, dates, figs, melons, and peaches are some of the fruits available. Almonds, walnuts, macadamia nuts, hazelnuts, cashews, sunflower seeds, pumpkin seeds, almond butter, and peanut butter are among the nuts, seeds, and nut butters available. Beans, peas, lentils, pulses, peanuts, and chickpeas are examples of legumes. Oats, brown rice, rye, barley, maize, buckwheat, whole wheat bread and pasta are all examples of whole grains. Salmon, sardines, trout, tuna, mackerel, shrimp, oysters, clams, crab, and mussels are examples of fish and seafood. Chicken, duck, and turkey are examples of poultry. Chicken, quail, and duck eggs are available. Cheese, yogurt, and milk are examples of dairy products.Garlic, basil, mint, rosemary, sage, nutmeg, cinnamon, and pepper are some of the herbs and spices used. Extra virgin olive oil, olives, avocados, and avocado oil are all good sources of healthy fats.

Which Food Should Be Avoided
When following the Mediterranean diet, you should avoid the following processed foods and ingredients:Added sugar can be found in a variety of foods, but it is particularly prevalent in soda, candies, ice cream, table sugar, syrup, and baked goods.White bread, tortillas, chips, and crackers are examples of refined grains.Margarine, fried foods, and other processed foods contain trans fats. Soybean oil, canola oil, cottonseed oil, and grapeseed oil are examples of refined oils. Meat that has been processed, such as sausages, hot dogs, deli meats, and beef jerky. Fast food, convenience meals, microwave popcorn, and granola bars are examples of highly processed foods.

Avocado Toast

Time to prepare: 10 minutes Time to cook: 0 minutes

Ingredients: For 2 People

- 1 tablespoon crumbled goat's cheese
- 1 peeled, pitted, and mashed avocado
- a sprinkle of black pepper and a pinch of salt
- 2 heated whole-wheat bread pieces
- half tbsp lime juice
- 1 finely sliced persimmon
- 1 finely sliced fennel bulb
- honey (two teaspoons)
- pomegranate seeds, 2 tblsp.

Preparation:

1. In a mixing bowl, whisk together the avocado flesh, salt, pepper, lime juice, and cheese.

2. Spread the mixture over toasted bread pieces and top with the other ingredients before serving for breakfast.

Serve with scrambled eggs as a side dish.

Choose ideally ripe avocados; unripe avocados are difficult to mash and have little taste.

Nutritional Values Per Serving:

348 calories | 20.8 g fat | 249 mg sodium | 38.7 g carbs | 12.3 g fiber | 37.4 g sugar | 7.1 g protein

Strawberry Smoothie Bowl

- Time to Prepare: 10 minutes

- Time to Cook 30 minutes

Ingredients: For 2 People

- 1 peeled banana, cut into bits

- 2 cups strawberries, frozen

- a third of a cup of whey protein powder

- 2 cups almond milk (unsweetened)

- 2 tbsp. acai powder (organic)

Preparation:

1. In a high-powered blender, add all of the ingredients and process until smooth.

2. Divide the mixture evenly between two serving dishes.

Before serving, sprinkle the granola, chia seeds, and banana slices over top.

Cinnamon may be substituted for cardamom in this recipe.

Per Serving Nutritional Values:

693 calories | 59.2 grams of fat | 52 grams of saturated fat | 41.4 grams of carbohydrates | 9.8 grams of fiber | 24.3 grams of sugar | 9.8 grams of protein

Almond Chia Porridge

Time to prepare: 10 minutes

Time to cook: 30 minutes to prepare

4 servings

Ingredients:

- 3 cups almond milk (organic)
- 1/3 cup dried chia seeds
- 1 teaspoon extract de vanille
- 14 teaspoon cardamom powder
- 1 tablespoon honey

Preparation:

1. Fill a pot halfway with almond milk and bring to a boil.

2. Remove the almond milk from the heat and set it aside to cool for 15 minutes.

3. Combine the vanilla extract, honey, and powdered cardamom in a mixing bowl. Stir everything together well.

4. Stir in the chia seeds one more.

5. Cover and let aside for 20–25 minutes to allow the chia seeds to absorb the liquid.

6. Spoon the cooked porridge into ramekins to serve.

Serve with fresh raspberries as a garnish.

Stir the chia seeds well to prevent lumps from developing.

Per Serving Nutritional Values:

444 calories | 43.6 g fat | 28 mg sodium | 15.4 g carbs | 4.7 g fiber | 10.5 g sugar | 4.5 g protein

Avocado Milkshake

Time to prepare: 5 minutes Time to Cook: 0 minutes

3 servings Ingredients:

- 1 peeled and pitted avocado
- 2 tablespoons honey (liquid)
- 1/2 teaspoon of vanilla extract
- 1/2 CUP HEAVY COOKER'S CREAM
- 1 cup of milk
- One third of a cup of ice cubes

Preparation:

1. Cut the avocado into small pieces and place it in a food processor.

2. Combine the liquid honey, vanilla extract, heavy cream, milk, and ice cubes in a large mixing bowl.

3. Blend the ingredients until it is completely smooth.

4. Pour the milkshake into tall glasses to serve.

Serve with pancakes or waffles as a side dish.

Vegan milkshakes may be made using almond or coconut milk.

Per Serving Nutritional Values:

291 calories | 22.1 g fat | 51 mg sodium | 22 g carbs | 4.5 g fiber | 15.6 g sugar | 4.4 g protein

Yogurt Bowl with Caramelized Figs

Time to Prepare: 10 minutes 7-minute cook time

4 servings Ingredients:

- 2 cups plain Greek yogurt
- 8 ounces fresh figs, halved
- 3 tablespoons honey
- a pinch of cinnamon powder
- 1/4 cup chopped pistachios

Preparation:

1. Melt 1 tablespoon of honey in a prepared pan over medium heat for approximately 2 minutes.

2. Place the figs cut sides down in the pan and simmer for approximately 5 minutes, or until caramelized.

3. Take the pan off the heat and leave it aside for 2–3 minutes.

4. Place the caramelized fig halves on top of each serving dish of yogurt.

5. Add the pistachios and cinnamon to the top.

6. Drizzle the remaining honey over each bowl and serve.

Serve with blueberries on top as a garnish.

You may add some orange zest as a variation.

Per Serving Nutritional Values:

276 calories | 2.3 g fat | 0.3 g saturated fat | 53.6 g carbohydrates | 6 g fiber | 43.7 g sugar | 14.7 g protein

Tomato Omelet

Time to Prepare: 10 minutes Time to Cook: 5 minutes

2 Serving Ingredients

- 4 big eggs

- 1/4 cup water

- To taste, season with salt and black pepper.

- 1/4 cup crumbled goat's cheese

- 1 sliced scallion

- 1 tablespoon extra virgin olive oil

- 1/4 cup chopped tomato

Preparation:

1. In a small mixing bowl, whisk together the eggs, water, salt, and black pepper.

2. In a nonstick skillet, heat the olive oil over medium-high heat until it melts.

3. Cook for approximately 2 minutes after whisking in the egg mixture.

4. Carefully turn the omelet and cook for a further 2 minutes, or until it is fully set.

5. Cover one side of the omelet with cheese, onions, and tomato.

6. Fold the omelet in half carefully and remove it from the burner.

7. Divide the mixture into two equal parts and serve.

Serve with toasted whole-wheat bread pieces as a side dish.

Feta cheese may be used instead of goat's cheese as a variation.

Per Serving Nutritional Values:

216 calories | 17 grams of fat | 7.6 grams of saturated fat | 2.3 grams of carbohydrates | 0.5 grams of fiber | 1.6 grams of sugar | 14.1 grams of protein

Raspberry Oats

Time to Prepare: 10 minutes

Time to prepare: 5 minutes,

1 person Ingredients:

- 1/4 teaspoon vanilla
- 1/2 cup fresh raspberries
- 3/4 cup almond milk, unsweetened
- 2 teaspoons chia seeds
- 1 teaspoon honey
- One third of a cup of rolled oats
- 1 teaspoon of salt

Directions:

1. Place raspberries in a mixing dish and mash with a fork.

2. Combine the mashed raspberries and the additional ingredients in a glass container and mix thoroughly.

3. Refrigerate the jar overnight after covering it with a lid.

Serving Suggestion: Drizzle a little milk over top and serve. Add one to two drops of almond extract as a variation. Per Serving Nutritional Values:

289 calories | 11.1 g fat | 296 mg sodium | 41.8 g carbs | 14.2 g fiber | 8.9 g sugar | 8.5 g protein Time to Prepare: 10 minutes

Eggs with Avocado

Time to Prepare: 20 minutes Time to Cook: 25 minutes

6 serving ingredients

- Cooking spray with olive oil
- 3 tablespoons feta cheese, crumbled
- 1 big avocado, peeled, half, and pitted
- 4 eggs, room temperature,
- salt and black pepper to taste

Preparation:

1. Preheat the oven to 400 degrees Fahrenheit.

2. Arrange two gratin plates on a baking sheet in a single layer. Place in the oven for around 10 minutes to heat up.

3. Cut each half of an avocado into six pieces.

4. Remove the plates from the oven and spray them with cooking spray.

5. Arrange avocado slices in each dish and break two eggs gently in each dish.

6. Add the feta cheese, salt, and black pepper to taste.

7. Bake for 15 minutes, or until the eggs are done to your liking.

8. Remove from the oven and serve immediately.

Serving Suggestion: Serve with a cup of hot tea or coffee. Cottage cheese may be used in lieu of the feta cheese. Per Serving Nutritional Values:

123 calories | 10.5 grams of fat | 3 grams of saturated fat | 3.3 grams of carbohydrates | 2.3 grams of fiber | 0.6 grams of sugar | 5 grams of protein

Breakfast Quinoa

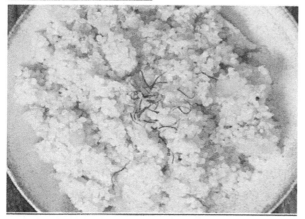

Time to prepare: 10 minutes

Time to prepare: 16 minutes

4 servings Ingredients:

- 12 teaspoon nutmeg
- 1 cup rinsed quinoa
- a pinch of cinnamon
- one third of a cup of flax seeds
- 12 cup almonds, sliced
- 12 cup chopped dried apricots
- 2 cups water

Directions:

1. In a saucepan, combine the quinoa and water and bring to a boil over medium heat.

2. Reduce to a low heat and continue to cook for 8-12 minutes, or until liquid has been absorbed.

3. Cook for 2-3 minutes after adding the nutmeg, cinnamon, flax seeds, almonds, and apricots.

Serve with a drizzle of milk as a finishing touch. Add a dash of honey if you want to make it sweeter. Per Serving Nutritional Values:287 calories | 11.7 g fat | 9 mg sodium | 35.2 g carbs | 7.8 g fiber | 2.5 g sugar | 10.5 g protein

Vegetable Egg Cups

Time to Prepare: 10 minutes

Time to Cook: 12 minutes

12servings ingredients:

- 6 quail eggs

- 1/4 cup unsweetened almond milk

- 2.7 ounces goat cheese, crumbled

- 1 $^{1/2}$ cups spinach, cut

- 1 red bell pepper,

- Salt

Directions:

1. Preheat the oven to 350 degrees Fahrenheit.

2. In a mixing dish, whisk together the eggs and milk.

3. Stir in the remaining ingredients well.

4. Pour the egg mixture into the buttered muffin tin and bake for 20 minutes in a preheated oven.

Allow time for the dish to cool fully before serving.

You may also use coconut milk as a variation.

Per Serving Nutritional Values:

76 calories | 5.7 g fat | 68 mg sodium | 1.5 g carbs | 0.3 g fiber | 1 g sugar | 5 g protein

Omelet Casserole

Preparation Time: 10 minutes

Time to Cook: 35 minutes

12 servings ingredients

- a dozen eggs

- 1 tablespoon extra virgin olive oil

- 1 teaspoon pepper (lemon)

- 1 teaspoon oregano, dry

- 2 cups almond milk

- 1 tablespoon dill, chopped

- 5 ounces sun-dried tomato, crumbled

- 12 ounces artichoke, drained and diced

- 1 teaspoon garlic, minced

- 1 teaspoon kosher salt

Directions:

1. Preheat the oven to 375 degrees Fahrenheit.

2. In a medium-sized skillet, heat the oil.

3. Add the garlic and spinach to the pan and cook for 3 minutes.

4. In a mixing dish, whisk together the eggs, milk, and salt. Sun-dried tomato, dill, oregano, lemon pepper, and sautéed spinach are all good additions.

5. Bake for 35 minutes after pouring the egg mixture into the oiled baking dish.

Allow time to cool fully before slicing and serving. Coconut milk may be used for almond milk in this recipe. Per Serving Nutritional Values:

210 calories | 16.9 g fat | 335 mg sodium | 9.4 g carbs | 3.7 g fiber | 2.1 g sugar | 8.6 g protein

Breakfast Chives Frittata

Time to Prepare: 10 minutes

Time to Cook:: 35 minutes

6 Servings ingredients

- 8 eggs, whisked

- 1 teaspoon crushed red pepper

- 2 minced garlic cloves

- 12 cup crumbled goat's cheese

- 2 tablespoons chives

- 2 tablespoons dill

- 4 diced tomatoes

- 1 tablespoon olive oil Season with salt and pepper to taste.

Directions:

1. Grease a baking pan and preheat the oven to 325 degrees Fahrenheit.

2. In a large mixing basin, thoroughly combine all of the ingredients and pour into the prepared pan.

3. Bake in the oven for 30–35 minutes, or until the centre is cooked through.

4. Take the dish out of the oven and serve.

Garnish with fresh chopped cilantro before serving. If you want a milder flavor, leave off the red pepper flakes. Per Serving Nutritional Values:

149 calories | 10.28 g fat | 210 mg sodium | 9.93 g carbs | 2.3 g fiber | 2 g sugar | 13.26 g protein

Spinach and Egg Scramble

Time to Prepare: 10 minutes

15 minutes Time to Cook:

1 person Ingredients:

- 1 tablespoon extra virgin olive oil

- $1^{1/2}$ cup spinach (baby)

- 2 eggs, to taste and beaten Kosher salt and black pepper

- 1/2 cup raspberries, chopped

- 1 slice whole-grain bread, toasted

Preparation:

1. In a nonstick skillet, heat the oil over medium-high heat.

2. Cook for 5–7 minutes after adding the spinach.

3. In the same skillet, crack the eggs and simmer for 5 minutes, stirring every 2 minutes.

4. Season with salt and pepper to taste.

5. Finally, serve and enjoy!

Serving Suggestion: Serve with toast and raspberries on top. Replace raspberries with your favorite fruit or avocado as a variation. Per Serving Nutritional Values:

296 calories | 16 g fat | 394 mg sodium | 21 g carbs | 7 g fiber | 5 g sugar | 18 g protein

Quinoa Porridge

Time to Prepare: 10 minutes 15 Time to Cook:

4 people Ingredients:

Directions:

- 1/2 cup washed quinoa

- 1 quart of water

- 1 cup rolled oats (gluten-free)

- 1/4 cup pumpkin seeds

- 1/2 cup unsweetened vanilla almond milk, plus more if required

- 14 cup chopped pecans

- 1 teaspoon of honey

Preparation:

1. Combine the quinoa and water in a small saucepan. Over medium heat, bring to a boil.

2. Reduce the heat to low and cook, uncovered, for 10–15 minutes, or until the liquid is absorbed. Allow to cool before serving.

3. Combine the chilled quinoa, oats, almond milk, pumpkin seeds, pecans, and honey in a medium mixing bowl.

4. Transfer to a storage container and keep refrigerated overnight, sealed.

5. Adjust the texture with extra almond milk in the morning if necessary. Serve.

Serve with blueberries and chopped nuts as a garnish.

Variation Tip: Use cooked quinoa instead than raw quinoa since raw quinoa has a bitter flavor.

Per Serving Nutritional Values:

282 calories | 9 g fat | 27 mg sodium | 42 g carbs | 5 g fiber | 5 g sugar | 10 g protein

Cheesy Potato Frittata

Time to Prepare: 10 minutes

Time to Cook:: 10 minutes

4 servings Ingredients:

Directions:

- 8 big eggs

- 1/3 Cup of milk

- a third of a cup of baby spinach

- 2 cups diced russet potatoes

- 3/4 cup sliced white onion

- 12 cup grated parmesan cheese

- 12 cup chopped fresh basil

- 2 teaspoons olive oil Season with salt and pepper to taste.

Preparation:

1. In a large mixing bowl, whisk together the eggs, milk, salt, and pepper.

2. In a pan over medium heat, combine the olive oil, potatoes, and chopped onion.

3. Cook until the onions are transparent, then add the spinach and cook until it begins to wilt, approximately a minute.

4. Pour the egg and milk mixture into the pan and sprinkle the parmesan cheese on top.

5. Cook the frittata for 5 minutes, or until the edges are golden brown.

Garnish with rosemary sprigs before serving.

Substitute kale for spinach as a variation.

Per Serving Nutritional Values:

281 calories | 17.9 g fat | 329 mg sodium | 15.9 g carbs | 2.4 g fiber | 3.5 g sugar | 15.5 g protein

Breakfast Hummus Toast

Time to Prepare: 10 minutes

Time to Cook: 5 minutes

4 servings ingredient:

- 4 toasted rye bread slices
- One third of a cup of hummus
- 1/4 cup mixed greens
- 1 tomato, sliced
- 1/2 cup chopped red onion
- 1 teaspoon salt and pepper

Preparation:

1. While the bread is toasting, prepare the cut veggies.

2. To make open-faced sandwiches, stack the hummus, tomatoes, onions, and mixed greens on the toasted bread.

3. Season to taste with salt and pepper.

Serve with chopped cilantro as a garnish.

Alternately, whole-wheat pita bread may be used instead of rye bread.

Per Serving Nutritional Values:

148 calories | 4.6 g fat | 261 mg sodium | 30.2 g carbs | 5.6 g fiber | 3.3 g sugar | 6.1 g protein

Creamy Millet

Time to Prepare: 10 minutes

15 minutes Time to Cook:

8 servings Ingredients:

- 2 cup of millet
- 1 cup unsweetened almond milk
- 1 quart of water
- 1 cup unsweetened coconut milk
- 1 teaspoon cinnamon powder
- 12 teaspoon ginger powder
- a quarter teaspoon of salt

- chia seeds, 1 tblsp.

- 1 tablespoon butter made from cashews

- 4 oz. coconut shredded

Preparation:

1. In a medium saucepan, combine the coconut milk, almond milk, and water; gently mix to combine.

2. Add the millet, stir thoroughly, and cover.

3. Cook for 5 minutes with the millet.

4. Stir in the chia seeds, cinnamon, ground ginger, and salt. Cook for another 5 minutes on medium heat, stirring constantly.

5. Cook for another 5 minutes after adding the cashew butter.

6. Transfer the mixture to serving dishes after removing it from the heat.

7. Finally, serve and enjoy.

Serve with a sprinkling of coconut.

Any nut butter may be substituted for cashew butter.

Per Serving Nutritional Values:

384 calories | 19.8 g fat | 215 mg sodium | 42.9 g carbs | 6.6 g fiber | 3.6 g sugar | 11.7 g protein

Cherry Oats Bowl

Time to Prepare: 10 minutes Time to cook: 0 minutes

1 person Ingredients:

- 1/2 cup rolled oats, organic
- 1/2 cup almond milk, unsweetened
- chia seeds, 1 tblsp.
- Hemp seeds, 1 teaspoon
- 2 teaspoons sliced almonds
- 1 tablespoon butter made from almonds
- 1 teaspoon extract de vanille
- 1/2 cup berries, fresh
- 1 cup cherries, frozen

44

- 1 cup Greek yogurt, plain

Preparation:

1. Soak the oats in unsweetened almond milk for 30 minutes.

2. Blend the soaked oats, frozen cherries, yogurt, chia seeds, almond butter, and vanilla extract until smooth.

extract.

3. Divide the mixture into two bowls.

4. Toss hemp seeds, sliced almonds, and fresh cherries into each dish in equal numbers.

Serve with a drizzle of honey as a finishing touch.

Variation Tip: You may use any milk instead of almond milk.

Per Serving Nutritional Values:

889 calories | 35.3 grams of fat | 126 milligrams of sodium | 112 grams of carbohydrates | 21.7 grams of fiber | 85.4 milligrams of sugar | 33.6 grams of protein

Oat and Berry Parfait

Time to Prepare: 10 minutes

Time to Cook: 12 minutes

2 servings ingredients:

- 1/2 cup rolled oats, whole grain
- 3/4 cup walnut pieces 1 tablespoon of honey
- 1 cup blueberries, fresh
- $1^{1/2}$ cup vanilla Greek yogurt (low-fat)
- Garnish with fresh mint leaves

Preparation:

1. Preheat the oven to 300 degrees Fahrenheit.

2. Arrange the oats and walnuts on a baking sheet in a single layer.

3. Toast the oats and almonds for 10 to 12 minutes, or until you can smell them cooking. Remove the baking sheet from the oven.

4. Heat the honey in a microwave-safe bowl until it's barely warm, approximately 30 seconds. Stir in the blueberries until they are evenly distributed.

5. In the bottom of two dessert dishes or 8-ounce glasses, place one spoonful of berries.

6. Add a layer of yogurt, followed by a layer of oats, and continue the layers until the containers are filled, finishing with the berries.

7. Serve.

Garnish with the mint leaves before serving. Substitute maple syrup for honey as a variation. Per Serving Nutritional Values:

916 calories | 35.8 g fat | 360 mg sodium | 115.7 g carbs | 7.6 g fiber | 90.9 g sugar | 39.9 g protein

Veggies and Egg Scramble

15-minute prep time

Time to cook: 8 minutes

2 servings ingredients

- 1 cup baby spinach, fresh

- 1 tablespoon extra virgin olive oil

- 1/3 cup sliced fresh tomato

- 2 tablespoons crumbled feta cheese

- 3 beaten eggs

- To taste, season with salt and black pepper.

Preparation:

1. In a large skillet over medium heat, heat the olive oil and sauté the tomatoes and spinach for approximately 4 minutes.

2. Add the eggs and cook, stirring constantly, for approximately 1 minute.

3. Add the feta cheese and simmer for another 2 minutes, or until the cheese has melted.

4. Remove from the fire and stir in the salt and black pepper.

5. Serve right away.

Serve with toasted whole-wheat bread as a side dish.

Fresh cilantro may also be used as a variation.

Per Serving Nutritional Values:

188 calories | 15.7 grams of fat | 4.5 grams of saturated fat | 2.6 grams of carbohydrates | 0.7 grams of fiber | 1.7 grams of sugar | 10.3 grams of protein

Yogurt with Berries and Nuts

Time to prepare:

5 minutes Time to cook: 0 minutes

1 person Ingredients:

- 6 oz. plain Greek yogurt (non-fat)

- 12 cup berries (fresh or frozen)

- 14 ounce walnuts, crushed

- 1 teaspoon of honey

Preparation:

1. Place the yogurt in a container with a cover.

2. Combine the berries, almonds, and honey in a mixing bowl.

3. Refrigerate for 2–3 days after sealing with the lid.

Garnish with mint before serving. Substitute maple syrup for honey as a variation. Per Serving Nutritional Values:

243 calories | 4.6 g fat | 136 mg sodium | 42.5 g carbs | 5.3 g fiber | 36 g sugar | 10.6 g protein

Eggs Florentine

Time to Prepare: 10 minutes

Time to Cook: 10 minutes

3 servings Ingredients:

- 2 tablespoons extra virgin olive oil
- 2 garlic cloves
- a third of a cup of cream cheese
- 12 cup of mushrooms
- 12 CUP FRESH SPROUTING SPROUTING SPROUTING S
- To taste, season with salt and black pepper.
- 6 quail eggs

Preparation:

1. In a non-stick skillet, heat the oil. Mix in the mushrooms and garlic for approximately 1 minute, or until the garlic is aromatic.

2. Add the spinach to the mushroom paste and simmer for 2–3 minutes, or until the spinach softens.

3. Mix the mushroom and spinach mixture together, then season with salt and pepper.

4. Add the eggs and heat, stirring constantly, until stiff; flip.

5. Pour the cream cheese over the egg mixture and heat for 5 minutes, or until the cheese begins to melt.

Serve with toasted bread pieces as a side dish.

Optional Seasoning: Feel free to add extra seasoning if desired.

Per Serving Nutritional Values:

278.9 calories | 22.9 g fat | 191 mg sodium | 4.1 g carbs | 22.9 g fiber | 1.1 g sugar | 15.7 g protein

Fruity Quinoa Bowl

15-minute prep time

15 minutes Time to Cook

Ingredients: Ingredients: Ingredients: Ingredients:
Ingredients: Ingredients:

- 1/2 cup unsweetened skim milk

- 1/2 teaspoon vanilla extract

- 1/2 cup rinsed and drained uncooked quinoa

- 1/2 cup of water

- 1/2 teaspoon cinnamon powder

- 1/2 cup chopped cashews

- 1/2 cup blackberries, fresh

- 1/2 CUP DRIED STRAWBERRIES

- 1 teaspoon of honey

Preparation:

1. Bring the milk, quinoa, water, and cinnamon to a boil in a preheated saucepan over medium heat.

2. Reduce the heat to low and cook, covered, for about 15 minutes, or until all of the liquid has been absorbed, stirring occasionally.

3. Stir in the cashews, cherries, and honey after removing the pan from the heat.

4. Evenly distribute the quinoa mixture into serving bowls.

5. Garnish with a blackberry topping.

Serving Suggestion: Before serving, drizzle with more honey.

Variation Tip: Blueberries and strawberries can be used in place of the blackberries.

Per Serving Nutritional Values:

477 calories | 18.6 grams of fat | 3.5 grams of saturated fat | 66.2 grams of carbohydrates | 6.8 grams of fiber | 24.7 grams of sugar | 13.8 grams of protein

White Bean Soup

Time to prepare: 10 minutes

Time to Cook:: 8 hours

6 minutes ingredients

- 6 cups vegetarian stock
- 1 cup celery, diced
- 1 cup carrot, chopped
- 1 yellow onion, chopped
- 2 cups navy beans, dried
- 1/2 teaspoon basil, dried
- 1/2 teaspoon sage, dried 1 teaspoon thyme, dried
- 4 garlic cloves, minced
- a sprinkle of black pepper
- and a pinch of salt

Preparation:

1. Combine the beans, stock, and the other ingredients in a slow cooker.

2. Cook on Low for 8 hours with the lid on.

3. Pour the soup into dishes and serve immediately.

Serve with roasted veggies and crusty bread as a side dish. Variation Tip: For a healthy outcome, add extra veggies of your choosing! Per Serving Nutritional Values:

264 calories | 17.5 g fat | 751 mg sodium | 23.7 g carbs | 4.5 g fiber | 6.6 g sugar | 11.5 g protein

Cucumber and Tomato Salad

Time to prepare: 10 minutes

Time to Cook: 0 minutes

4 servings Ingredients:

- To taste, season with salt and black pepper.

- 1 tablespoon lemon juice, freshly squeezed

- 1 chopped onion

- 1 peeled and diced cucumber

- 2 diced tomatoes

- 4 cups spinach

Preparation:

1. Combine the onions, cucumbers, and tomatoes in a salad dish.

2. Season with salt and pepper to taste.

3. Stir in the lemon juice well.

4. Mix in the spinach, toss to coat, and serve.

Serve with feta cheese and chickpeas as a garnish.

Remove the seeds from the cucumber if you don't want the cucumber to be bitter.

Per Serving Nutritional Values:

70.3 calories | 0.3 g fat | 50 mg sodium | 8.9 g carbs | 2.4 g fiber | 4.3 g sugar | 2.2 g protein

Lentil Soup

Time to Prepare: 10 minutes

Time to Cook: 35 minutes

4 servings Ingredients:

- 1 tablespoon extra virgin olive oil
- 1 chopped onion
- 2 chopped celery stalks
- 1 tablespoon minced garlic
- 6 mugs vegetable stock with minimal sodium
- 2 cans low-sodium diced tomatoes (28 oz.)
- 1 (15-ounce) can washed and drained low-sodium red lentils
- 1 tblsp basil leaves, chopped
- 1 tsp. red pepper flakes
- to taste with sea salt and black pepper

Preparation:

1. Heat the olive oil in a saucepan over medium-high heat.

2. Saute the onion, celery, and garlic for 3 minutes, or until softened.

3. Bring the stock, salt, and pepper, as well as the tomatoes and their juices, to a boil.

4. Reduce the heat to low and continue to cook for another 20 minutes.

5. Puree the contents in a food processor until it is smooth.

6. Return the broth to the pot, add the lentils, basil, and red pepper flakes, and cook for approximately 10 minutes, stirring occasionally.

7. Serve.

Serve with toasted whole-wheat bread as a side dish.

Variation: Use chicken stock instead of vegetable stock.

Per Serving Nutritional Values:

211 calories | 4 g fat | 336 mg sodium | 36 g carbs | 13 g fiber | 11 g sugar | 12 g protein

Cauliflower and Farro Salad

Time to Prepare: 20 minutes

4 servings Ingredients:

To make the salad

- 3/4 cup farro pearled
- Add to taste kosher salt
- 2 tablespoons extra virgin olive oil
- 1 medium cauliflower head, divided into bite-sized florets
- 1/2 medium red onion, thinly sliced
- 1/4 cup fresh parsley
- 1 oz. shaved parmesan cheese

To prepare the dressing

- 2 tblsp. freshly squeezed lemon juice
- 3 tbsp extra-virgin extra-virgin olive oil
- 1 tblsp. tahini sauce
- 12 tsp. kosher salt
- 1 minced tiny garlic clove

Preparation:

1. Preheat a skillet over medium-high heat. Toast the farro for 5 minutes, or until nutty and browned, stirring the pan regularly.

2. Pour in enough water to cover the farro by about a half-inch, season with salt, and bring to a boil.

3. Cook, stirring occasionally, for approximately 25 minutes, or until the farro is soft but still chewy.

4. Using a fine mesh strainer, sift the farro.

5. Place the farro in a large mixing basin and put aside to cool somewhat.

6. In a pan over medium-high heat, heat the olive oil and sauté the cauliflower for approximately 6 minutes, turning constantly.

7. Add the onion and cook for approximately 3 minutes, stirring occasionally.

8. Take the pan from the heat and put it aside.

9. To make the dressing, whisk together all of the dressing ingredients in a mixing bowl until smooth.

10. Toss the farro, dressing, and cauliflower combination together in a large serving dish.

11. Garnish with parsley and parmesan cheese before serving.

Serve with your favorite main meal as a side dish. You may also add some rosemary to this salad as a variation. Per Serving Nutritional Values:

286 calories | 14.3 grams of fat | 2.9 grams of saturated fat | 33.1 grams of carbohydrates | 6.7 grams of fiber | 4.3 grams of sugar | 10.6 grams of protein

Greek Chicken Gyro Salad

Time to prepare: 10 minutes

7-Minute Cooking Time

Ingredients 4 servings

Chicken

- 3 tablespoons oregano (dried)

- 2 tablespoons extra virgin olive oil

- 1 tablespoon vinegar (red wine)

- Boneless chicken breasts, 1.1/4 pound

- 1 teaspoon black pepper, ground

- a quarter-cup of lemon juice

- 1 tsp. salt (kosher)

Salad

- 6 cups lettuce

- 1 cup English cucumber, diced

- 1 cup diced feta cheese

- 1 cup diced tomatoes

- 1/2 cup sliced red onion

- 1 cup crumbled pita chips

Tzatziki is a Greek yogurt sauce.

- 1 tablespoon vinegar (white)

- a quarter teaspoon of kosher salt

- Greek yogurt, 8 oz.

- 2/3 cup English cucumber,

- grated 1 garlic clove,

- minced a quarter-cup of lemon juice

- 3/4 teaspoon black pepper,

- ground 2 tsp. dill weed, dried

- a little amount of sugar

Preparation:

1. In a pan over medium heat, heat the oil, then add the chicken, salt, oregano, and black pepper.

2. Cook for a total of five minutes.

3. Reduce the heat to low and add the lemon juice and vinegar, then continue to cook for another five minutes.

4. Cook until the chicken is fully cooked. Remove the pan from the heat and put it aside after the chicken is done.

5. In a large serving dish, combine the tomatoes, pita chips, chicken, lettuce, cucumber, and onions. Combine all ingredients and put aside. The salad has been prepared.

6. In a separate dish, combine the yogurt, cucumber, garlic, lemon juice, vinegar, dill, salt, pepper, and sugar. Mix

well. The sauce has been prepared.

Serve the salad with the sauce on top and the roasted chicken on the side.

Variation Tip: For a better finish, marinate your chicken ahead of time.

Per Serving Nutritional Values:

737 calories | 29 grams of fat | 1253 milligrams of sodium | 54 grams of carbohydrates | 6 grams of fiber | 5.7 milligrams of sugar | 64 grams of protein

Pecan Salmon Salad

Time to Prepare: 10 minutes

Time to cook: 0 minutes

4 servings Ingredients:

- 6 cups baby greens (mixed) (spinach, kale, and Swiss chard)
- 2 big peeled oranges, cut into bits
- 2 peeled and cut into bits red grapefruits
- 1 peeled, pitted, and chopped avocado
- 2 drained 5-ounce cans boneless, skinless salmon
- 1/2 cup halved pecans
- 1/2 cup vinaigrette de pesto

Preparation:

1. Toss the greens with the oranges, grapefruits, avocado, salmon, and pecans on a large dish.

2. Drizzle the vinaigrette over the salad and serve.

Serve with chopped cilantro as a garnish.

Swap the pecans with sunflower or pumpkin seeds as a variation.

Per Serving Nutritional Values:

459 calories | 34 grams of fat | 191 milligrams of sodium | 28 grams of carbohydrates | 8 grams of fiber | 13 grams of sugar | 19 grams of protein

Lebanese Bean Salad

Time to prepare: 2 hours and 10 minutes

Time to cook: 0 minutes

5 servings Ingredients:

- 1 (15-ounce) can drained and washed fava beans

- 1 can (15 oz.) chickpeas, washed and drained

- 1 can (1512-ounce) drained and washed white beans

- 1/4 cup chopped flat-leaf parsley

- 3 teaspoons olive oil

- 1 lemon, juiced

- 2 garlic cloves, minced Kosher salt and black pepper, to taste

Preparation:

1. In a mixing basin, thoroughly combine all of the ingredients.

2. Marinate for two hours in the refrigerator.

3. Finally, serve and enjoy!

Serve with fresh cilantro on top as a garnish. Add a pinch of spice with chili flakes as a variation. Per Serving Nutritional Values:

312 calories | 9.3 g fat | 418 mg sodium | 44.7 g carbs | 10 g fiber | 1.5 g sugar | 13.2 g protein

Spicy Tomato Soup

15-minute prep time

Time to Cook:: 28 minutes

8 servings Ingredients:

2 finely sliced medium yellow onions

3 tablespoons extra virgin olive oil

season with salt to taste

1 teaspoon cumin powder

1/2 teaspoon crushed red pepper flakes

1 can (28 oz.) plum tomatoes with liquids that are low in sodium

1/2 cup crumbled ricotta cheese curry powder (three tablespoons)

1 teaspoon cilantro powder

1 can (15 oz.) tomatoes chopped in a low-sodium sauce with juice

5.1/2 cup vegetable broth (low sodium)

Preparation:

1. Heat the olive oil, onions, and 1 teaspoon of salt in a large wok over medium-low heat.

2. Cook for approximately 12 minutes, stirring periodically.

3. Cook for 1 minute after adding the curry powder, cilantro, cumin, and red pepper flakes.

4. Add the broth and all of the tomatoes, together with their juices, and cook for 15 minutes.

5. Remove the soup from the heat and puree with a hand blender until smooth.

6. Serve immediately with ricotta cheese on top.

Serve with mozzarella sticks as a side dish. Ricotta cheese may be substituted with feta cheese as a variation. Per Serving Nutritional Values:

120 calories | 6.7 grams of fat | 1.5 grams of saturated fat | 9.8 grams of carbohydrates | 1.3 grams of fiber | 2.6 grams of sugar | 5 grams of protein

Cheesy Beet Soup

Time to Prepare: 10 minutes

30 minutes Time to Cook:

4 servings Ingredients:

- 1 tablespoon extra virgin olive oil
- 6 big peeled and sliced beets
- 6 cups low-sodium chicken stock
- 1 fennel bulb, finely chopped
- 1 sweet onion, diced
- 1 teaspoon garlic, minced
- 1/2 cup crumbled goat's cheese, sea salt and black pepper to taste
- 1 tablespoon chopped fresh parsley

Preparation:

1. Heat the olive oil in a saucepan over medium-high heat.

2. Cook, stirring occasionally, until the beets, fennel, onion, and garlic are softened, about 10 minutes.

3. Bring the soup to a boil with the chicken stock.

4. Reduce the heat to low and cook for 20 minutes, or until the veggies are very soft.

5. Puree the soup in a food processor or with an immersion blender until completely smooth.

6. Season the soup with salt and pepper and return it to the saucepan.

7. Serve.

Serve with a dollop of goat's cheese and a sprig of parsley on top. Variation: Vegetable stock may be used instead of chicken stock. Per Serving Nutritional Values:

309 calories | 13 grams of fat | 1984 milligrams of sodium | 32 grams of carbohydrates | 5 grams of fiber | 17 grams of sugar | 17 grams of protein

Mediterranean Watermelon Salad

Time to prepare: 10 minutes

Time to Cook:: 0 minutes

6 servings ingredients

- 6 cups torn mixed salad greens

- 3 cups seeded and cubed watermelon

- 1/2 cup sliced onion

- 1 tbsp extra-virgin extra-virgin olive oil

- 13 cup crumbled feta cheese

- to taste cracked black pepper

Preparation:

1. Combine all of the ingredients in a large mixing bowl.

2. Toss everything together well.

3. Allow chilling before serving.

Serving Suggestion: Serve with your favorite barbequed meat.

Avocado slices can be added for a creamier result.

Per Serving Nutritional Values:

Calories 91| Fat 4.3g | Sodium 130mg | Carbs 11.4g | Fiber 0.5g | Sugar 5.4g | Protein 3.5g

Chickpea, Bean, and Veggie Salad
Time to Prepare: 20 minutes

6 servings ingredients

- 1 (15-ounce) can rinsed and drained low-sodium black beans

- 1/4 cup fresh cilantro, chopped

- 2 cups fresh cherry tomatoes, halved

- 2 tbsp lime juice, freshly squeezed

- 1 (15-ounce) can rinsed and drained low-sodium chickpeas

- a quarter teaspoon of red chili powder

- 1/4 cup crumbled feta cheese

- 2 peeled, pitted, and chopped medium avocados

- 1 low-sodium corn can (15 ounces), rinsed and drained

- 1 drained (214-ounce) can diced olives

- 2 tbsp extra-virgin extra-virgin olive oil

- 1/4 teaspoon salt

- 1 teaspoon cumin powder

Preparation:

1. In a large mixing bowl, combine the chickpeas, maize, beans, olives, avocados, and tomatoes.

2. In a separate bowl, combine the remaining ingredients (except the feta cheese) until well combined.

3. Toss the salad with the dressing to evenly coat it.

4. Garnish with feta cheese before serving.

You might also add some sliced onion as a garnish.

Cilantro may be substituted with parsley as a variation.

Per Serving Nutritional Values:

573 calories | 23.3 grams of fat | 4.5 grams of saturated fat | 75.4 grams of carbohydrates | 23.3 grams of fiber | 13 grams of sugar | 22.9 grams of protein

Zucchini and Basil Soup
15-minute prep time

Time to Cook:

- 25 minutes Ingredients:
- 6 servings ingredients
- 2 teaspoons olive oil
- 2.1/2 pound zucchini, chopped
- 1/3 cup fresh basil leaves, chopped
- 1 medium onion, chopped
- 4 garlic cloves, chopped
- 1/3 cup heavy cream
- 4 quarts chicken stock
- To taste, season with salt and black pepper.
- 2 tbsp extra-virgin extra-virgin olive oil

Preparation:

1. Combine the olive oil, zucchini, and onion in a large skillet over medium-low heat.

2. Cook for approximately 6 minutes, stirring often.

3. Add the garlic and cook for another minute.

4. Pour in the chicken broth and bring to a boil over high heat.

5. Lower the heat to medium-low and continue to cook for another 15 minutes.

6. Remove from the heat and add the basil, salt, and black pepper.

7. Using an immersion blender, puree the soup until it is smooth.

8. To serve, ladle the soup into serving bowls and top with extra-virgin olive oil.

9. Drizzle with heavy cream and serve right away.

Serve with toasted whole-wheat bread slices as a side dish. Vegetable broth can be substituted for chicken broth in this recipe. Per Serving Nutritional Values:

170 calories | 13.1 grams of fat | 3.2 grams of saturated fat | 9.6 grams of carbohydrates | 2.5 grams of fiber | 4.5 grams of sugar | 6 grams of protein

Carrot Soup

Time to Prepare: 10 minutes

Time to Cook: 25 minutes

2 people Ingredients:

- 12 onion, chopped
- 2 teaspoons fresh ginger, minced
- 1 teaspoon fresh garlic, minced
- 4 cups water
- 3 carrots, chopped
- 1 teaspoon turmeric powder
- 12 cup coconut milk
- 1 tablespoon chopped fresh cilantro
- 1 tablespoon extra virgin olive oil

Preparation:

1. In a medium saucepan, heat the olive oil.

2. Soften the onion, garlic, and ginger in a skillet (3 minutes). Combine the water, carrots, and turmeric in a mixing bowl.

3. Bring the mixture to a boil, then reduce to a low heat and cook until the carrots are tender, about 15 minutes (20 minutes).

4. Pour the soup into a blender, along with the coconut milk, and blend until smooth.

Serving Suggestion: Garnish the soup with cilantro before serving.

Variation Tip: Vegetable broth can be used instead of water.

Per Serving Nutritional Values:

259 calories | 21.6 g fat | 89 mg sodium | 17.4 g carbs | 4.7 g fiber | 7.8 g sugar | 2.8 g protein

Portuguese Salad

Time to Prepare: 10 minutes

Time to cook: 0 minutes

4 servings Ingredients:

- 1 iceberg lettuce head, cleaned, dried, and ripped into pieces
- 4 sliced medium tomatoes
- 1 shredded medium carrot
- 1 sliced small cucumber
- 1 seeded and finely sliced tiny green bell pepper
- 1 onion, sliced into rings
- 12 cup olives, pitted (black or green) To serve, lemon wedges
- Garnish with chopped fresh parsley

To make the dressing, combine the following ingredients.

- 2 tablespoons extra virgin olive oil
- 2 tbsp balsamic vinegar or red wine vinegar
- Season with salt and pepper to taste.

Preparation:

1. In a small dish, whisk together the dressing ingredients and put aside.

2. Toss the lettuce with the tomatoes, carrots, cucumber, green bell pepper, onion, and olives in a serving dish.

3. Drizzle the dressing over top.

Serving Suggestion: Serve with lemon wedges and chopped parsley as a garnish.

Crisphead lettuce may be used instead of iceberg lettuce as a variation.

Per Serving Nutritional Values:

141 calories | 8.6 g fat | 260 mg sodium | 16.1 g carbs | 4.4 g fiber | 8.9 g sugar | 3 g protein

Quinoa MangoSalad

Time to Prepare: 10 minutes

Time to prepare: 20 minutes

4 people servings ingredients

- 1 cup dry quinoa

- 1 cucumber, sliced

- 1 ripe mango, peeled and diced

- 2 pints cherry or grape tomatoes, halved

- 1/4 cup fresh basil leaves, coarsely chopped

- 2 teaspoons balsamic vinegar

- 1.1/2 cup cooked garbanzo beans

- 5 oz of mixed baby green mixed together

Preparation:

1. Place the quinoa in a fine-mesh strainer and rinse for a few seconds under lukewarm water.

2. In a saucepan, bring 2 cups of water to a boil.

3. Stir in the quinoa and turn the heat down to medium.

4. Cover and cook for approximately 15 minutes, or until all of the liquid has evaporated.

5. In a large mixing bowl, combine the cooked quinoa, cucumber, mango, onion, basil, vinegar, and beans.

6. Serve on a bed of mixed greens.

Garnish with fresh parsley before serving.

Substitute two fresh peaches, pitted and chopped, for the mango.

Per Serving Nutritional Values:

335 calories | 3.3 grams of fat | 39 milligrams of sodium | 65 grams of carbohydrates | 10.6 grams of fiber | 12.1 grams of sugar | 15 grams of protein

Beets and Walnut Salad
Time to Prepare: 10 minutes

Time to Cook: 10 minutes

3 servings Ingredients:

- beets, 2 oz.

- arugula, 3 oz.

- Bibb lettuce, 2 oz.

- romaine lettuce, 9 oz.

- 1/4 cup breadcrumbs, dry

- 1/4 tbsp thyme (dry)

- 1/4 tbsp basil (dry)

- 1 teaspoon cayenne pepper

- goat's cheese,

- 6 oz (preferably in log shape)

- a quarter-cup of walnuts

- 1/4 cup vinaigrette de vin rouge

1. Preheat the oven to 425 degrees Fahrenheit.

2. Prepare all of the salad greens by trimming, washing, and drying them. Toss the greens thoroughly after tearing them into tiny bits.

3. Combine the herbs, pepper, and crumbs in a mixing bowl.

4. Cut the cheese into 1-ounce pieces with a sharp knife. To coat the cheese slices, roll them in the seasoned crumbs mixture.

5. Spread the cheese out on a baking sheet.

6. Bake for 10 minutes at 350°F.

7. Meanwhile, toast the walnuts with the cheese in a dry sauté pan or in the oven.

8. Toss the greens with the vinaigrette and serve immediately.

Serve by sprinkling walnuts on top of two slices of cheese on each dish of greens.

Fresh thyme and basil may be used instead of dried thyme and basil.

Per Serving Nutritional Values:

460 calories | 40 grams of fat | 787 milligrams of sodium | 21.4 grams of carbohydrates | 2 grams of fiber | 9.1 grams of sugar | 17 grams of protein

Moroccan Chickpea Soup

Time to Prepare: 10 minutes

Time to Cook:: 40 minutes

6 people servings ingredients

- 1/4 cup chopped fresh parsley or mint
- 1/4 teaspoon cumin
- 1/4 teaspoon crushed ginger
- 1/4 teaspoon saffron threads, broken
- 1/2 teaspoon hot paprika
- 1 onion, finely chopped
- 1 (1412-ounce) can diced tomatoes
- 1 pound unpeeled red potatoes, cut into
- 12-inch pieces
- 1 teaspoon sugar
- 1 zucchini, cut into 12-inch pieces
- 2 (15-ounce) cans rinsed garbanzo beans
- 3 tablespoons extra-virgin olive oil
- 312 cup chicken or vegetable broth
- 4 garlic cloves, minced
- Season with salt and pepper to taste.

Preparation:

1. In a Dutch oven, heat the oil over medium to high heat until it begins to shimmer.

2. Add the onion, sugar, and 12 tsp salt and simmer for 5 minutes, or until the onion softens.

3. Add the garlic, paprika, saffron, ginger, and cumin and simmer for about half a minute, or until fragrant.

4. Combine the beans, potatoes, tomatoes with their juice, zucchini, and broth in a large mixing bowl.

5. Reduce to a low heat and cook, stirring occasionally, for 20 to 30 minutes, or until the potatoes are cooked.

6. To thicken the soup, mash some potatoes against the pot's side with a wooden spoon.

7. Remove from heat, stir in the parsley or mint, and season to taste with salt and pepper.

Serve with lemon wedges as an accompaniment. Variation: Vegetable stock may be used instead of chicken stock. Per Serving Nutritional Values:

120 calories | 26.9 grams of fat | 276 milligrams of sodium | 105.5 grams of carbohydrates | 28 grams of fiber | 19.8 grams of sugar | 135.1 grams of protein

Roasted Tomato Basil Soup

Time to Prepare: 10 minutes

Time to Cook: 50 minutes

6 Serving ingredients

- 3 pounds halved Roma tomatoes
- Olive oil
- 2 carrots, chopped
- Salt and black pepper to taste
- 2 yellow onions, chopped
- 5 garlic cloves, minced
- 2 ounces basil leaves
- 1 cup crushed tomatoes
- 3 thyme sprigs
- 1 teaspoon dry oregano
- 2.1/2 teaspoon thyme leaves
- 1/2 teaspoon cumin
- 1 tablespoon lemon juice

Preparation:

1. In a mixing bowl, combine the salt, olive oil, carrot, black pepper, and tomatoes.

2. Transfer the carrot mixture to a baking dish and bake for 30 minutes at 450°F in a preheated oven.

3. In a blender, puree the baked mixture. During the mixing process, you may add a splash of water if necessary.

4. In a saucepan, sauté the onions in olive oil for three minutes over medium heat.

5. Add the garlic and cook for a further minute.

6. Add the crushed tomatoes, water, spices, thyme, salt, basil, and pepper to the blended tomato mixture in the saucepan.

7. Bring the mixture to a boil. Reduce the heat to low and continue to cook for another 20 minutes.

8. Finish with a squeeze of lemon juice and serve.

Serve with bread pieces as a side dish.

Variation Tip: For a hotter flavor, add chili.

Per Serving Nutritional Values:

104 calories | 0.8 g fat | 117 mg sodium | 23.4 g carbs | 5.4 g fiber | 8.5 g sugar | 4.3 g protein

Quinoa and Veggie Salad

Time to Prepare: 20 minutes Time to Cook: 20 minutes

8 servings Ingredients:

- 1.1/2 cup rinsed and drained dry quinoa To taste, season with salt and black pepper.

- 1 tblsp balsamic vinaigrette

- 1 (15-ounce) can low-sodium garbanzo beans, washed and drained

- 1/2 teaspoon dry thyme, crushed

- 1/3 cup drained and sliced roasted red bell pepper

- 1/4 cup finely sliced fresh basil

- 1/2 cup extra-virgin olive oil

- 3 cups water

- 1/2 teaspoon dry basil, crushed

- 2 small garlic cloves, pressed

- 3 cups arugula (fresh)

- 1/3 cup pitted and sliced fresh Kalamata olives

- 1/3 cup crumbled feta cheese

Preparation:

1. Bring a pot of water to a boil, then add the quinoa and 12 teaspoon of salt. Over high heat, bring to a boil.

2. Lower the heat to low, cover, and cook for 20 minutes, or until all of the liquid has been absorbed.

3. Remove from the heat and fluff the quinoa with a fork.

4. Allow to cool fully before serving.

5. To make the dressing, whisk together the olive oil, garlic, vinegar, dried herbs, salt, and black pepper in a mixing bowl.

6. In a large serving bowl, combine the garbanzo beans, quinoa, arugula, bell pepper, olives, and feta cheese.

7. Toss the salad with the dressing to evenly coat it.

8. Garnish with the dried basil before serving.

Serve alongside your favorite meal as a side dish.

Variation Tip: You can use any type of bean you want.

Per Serving Nutritional Values:

304 calories Carbohydrates: 31.3g | Fiber: 2.7g | Sugar: 3.2g | Protein: 8.3g | Fat: 16.9g | Sat Fat: 3g | Carbohydrates: 31.3g | Fiber: 2.7g | Sugar: 3.2g

Spicy Lentil Soup

Time to Prepare: 20 minutes

Time to Cook: 1 hour 15 minutes

6 people Ingredients:

- 2 peeled and sliced carrots
- 2 tablespoons extra virgin olive oil
- 1 (14.1/2-ounce) can low-sodium diced tomatoes
- 2 celery stalks, chopped
- 3 garlic cloves, minced
- 1/4 teaspoon oregano (crushed)
- 1 teaspoon cumin powder
- 1/2 tbsp. paprika
- 3 cups chopped fresh spinach
- 2 tblsp. freshly squeezed lemon juice
- To taste, season with salt and black pepper.
- 1/4 teaspoon dried basil, crushed
- 1/4 teaspoon dried thyme, crushed
- 1/2 teaspoon powdered cilantro
- 2 sweet onions, minced
- 1.1/2 cup brown lentils, picked over and washed

- 6 cups vegetable broth (low sodium)

Preparation:

1. Place the carrots, celery, and onion in a large soup pan over medium heat.

2. After approximately 5 minutes, add the garlic and cook for another 5 minutes.

3. After 1 minute of sautéing, add the brown lentils and stir-fry for 3 minutes.

4. Bring the mixture to a boil with the tomatoes, herbs, spices, and broth.

5. Reduce the heat to low and cook for approximately 1 hour, slightly covered.

6. Cook for 4 minutes after adding the spinach, salt, and black pepper.

7. Add the lemon juice and serve immediately.

Suggestions for Serving: Serve the soup with your favorite rice.

Yellow lentils may also be used as a variation.

Per Serving Nutritional Values:

128 calories | 5.1 grams of fat | 0.7 grams of saturated fat | 14.9 grams of carbohydrates | 3 grams of fiber | 4.5 grams of sugar | 5.7 grams of protein

Grilled Veggie Sandwich
Time to Prepare: 25 minutes

Time to Cook: 5 minutes

4 servings Ingredients:

- a quarter cup of mayonnaise Cooking spray with olive oil

- 1/2 teaspoon freshly squeezed lemon juice

- 2 thinly sliced zucchinis, lengthwise

- 2 portobello mushrooms, sliced thickly into 1/4-inch slices season with salt to taste

- 1/2 cup crumbled feta cheese

- 2 cups baby arugula, fresh

- 2 minced garlic cloves

- 1 eggplant, sliced thickly into 1/4-inch slices 14 of a ciabatta bread, divided horizontally

- 2 teaspoons olive oil

- 2 medium tomatoes, peeled and sliced

Preparation:

1. Preheat the oven to broil and coat a baking pan with cooking spray.

2. Toss the mayonnaise, garlic, and lemon juice together in a mixing basin. Remove from the equation.

3. Drizzle olive oil over the zucchini, eggplant, and mushrooms and season with salt.

4. Arrange the vegetable slices on a baking sheet and broil for 1.1/2 minutes on each side.

5. Arrange the vegetable pieces on a serving platter.

6. Place the loaves cut side down on the broiler rack and cook for approximately 2 minutes.

7. Remove each half-loaf from the broiler and cut into four equal-sized pieces.

8. Spread the mayonnaise mixture equally on each piece of bread, then layer on the vegetable slices, tomatoes, arugula, and feta cheese.

9. Place the top pieces on top and serve.

Serve these sandwiches with your favorite dip as a side dish.

Any species of mushroom may be used as a variation.

Per Serving Nutritional Values:

268 calories | 16.9 grams of fat | 8.3 grams of saturated fat | 25 grams of carbohydrates | 6.2 grams of fiber | 8.7 grams of sugar | 7.4 grams of protein

Bruschetta

Time to Prepare: 10 minutes

Time to Cook: 15 minutes

24 servings Ingredients:

- 6 pitted and chopped kalamata olives

- 2 tablespoons minced green onion

- 1/4 cup grated parmesan cheese, split

- 1/4 cup extra-virgin olive oil (or as required) for brushing

- 1/4 cup finely sliced cherry tomatoes

- 1 tsp lemon extract

- 1 tbsp extra-virgin extra-virgin olive oil

- 1 tablespoon pesto (basil)

- 1 halved and seeded red bell pepper

- 1 item (12 inches) 1/2 inch thick pieces of whole-wheat baguette

- a single packet (4 ounces) crumbled feta cheese with basil and sun-dried tomatoes

- 1 garlic clove, minced

Preparation:

1. Preheat the oven to 350°F and position the oven rack 6 inches below the heat source.

2. Brush 1/4 cup olive oil on both sides of the baguette pieces.

3. Arrange the bread pieces on a baking sheet and toast for approximately 1 minute on each side, keeping an eye on them to prevent them from burning.

4. Remove the toasted pieces and place them on a separate baking sheet.

5. Place the red peppers cut sides down on a baking sheet and broil for 8 to 10 minutes, or until the skin is browned and blistered.

6. Place the roasted peppers in a dish and wrap them in plastic wrap.

7. Remove the charred peel off the peppers when they have cooled. Remove the peel from the roasted peppers and cut them.

8. In a large mixing bowl, combine the roasted red peppers, cherry tomatoes, feta cheese, green onion, olives, pesto, 1 tablespoon olive oil, garlic, and lemon juice.

9. Spread one spoonful of the roasted pepper mixture on each slice of bread and gently sprinkle with parmesan cheese.

10. Broil for 2 minutes, or until gently browned on top.

Serve with chopped green onions and fresh basil as a garnish. Switch out the whole-wheat baguette with whole-wheat sourdough as a variation. Per Serving Nutritional Values:

73 calories | 4.8 g fat | 188 mg sodium | 5.3 g carbs | 0.2 g fiber | 0.4 g sugar | 2.1 g protein

Avocado Caprese Wrap

Time to prepare: 10 minutes

Time to Cook: 0 minutes

2 servings ingredients:

- 2 tortillas

- balsamic vinegar as required

- 1/2 cup arugula 1 mozzarella cheese ball, shredded

- 2 tablespoons fresh basil leaves, chopped Kosher salt to taste

- 1 tomato, sliced

- 1 avocado, thinly sliced

- Olive oil, to taste

- Add to taste black pepper

Preparation:

1. Evenly distribute the tomato pieces and cheese between the tortilla wrappers. After that, toss in the avocado and basil.

2. Drizzle olive oil and balsamic vinegar over top.

3. Add salt and pepper to taste.

4. Wrap the tortilla in plastic wrap and serve.

Garnish with parsley before serving.

Add chicken or fish for an even more delectable snack!

Per Serving Nutritional Values:

791 calories | 47 grams of fat | 280 milligrams of sodium | 71 grams of carbohydrates | 16 grams of fiber | 5.5 milligrams of sugar | 23 grams of protein

Zucchini Fritters

Time to prepare: 10 minutes

30 minutes cooking time

6 servings ingredients:

- 2 peeled and shredded zucchinis
- 1 thinly diced sweet onion
- 2 garlic cloves, minced
- 1/2 teaspoon fine sea salt 1 cup minced fresh parsley
- 1/2 tsp. black pepper
- 1/2 teaspoon allspice powder
- 2 tablespoons extra virgin olive oil
- 4 big eggs

Preparation:

1. Prepare a plate by lining it with paper towels and setting it aside.

2. In a large mixing bowl, combine the onion, parsley, garlic, zucchini, pepper, allspice, and sea salt.

3. Beat the eggs in a separate dish before adding them to the zucchini mixture. Make sure everything is fully combined.

4. Melt the butter in a large pan over medium heat.

5. Heat the olive oil, then spoon 1/4 cup of the mixture into the skillet at a time to make the fritters.

6. Cook for three minutes, or until the bottom of the pan has set.

7. Cook for another three minutes on the other side.

8. Drain the fritters by placing them on the prepared platter.

9. Serve.

Serve with pita bread as a side dish.

You may make this recipe dairy-free by omitting the eggs.

Per Serving Nutritional Values:

103 calories | 8 g fat | 216 mg sodium | 5 g carbs | 1.5 g fiber | 2.3 g sugar | 5 g protein

Carrot Cake Balls

Time to prepare: 10 minutes

Time to Cook: 10 minutes

22 servings Ingredients:

- 1/2 cup rolled oats, old-fashioned
- 1/4 teaspoon turmeric
- 1 cup pitted dates
- 1/2 teaspoon cinnamon powder
- 1 teaspoon vanilla extract
- 14 cup chia seeds
- 2 medium carrots, shredded
- 1/4 cup chopped pecans
- 1/4 teaspoon salt

Directions:

1. In a food processor, blend the dates, chia seeds, pecans, and oats until thoroughly incorporated.

2. Combine the remaining ingredients in a food processor and pulse until smooth.

3. Roll the oat mixture into tiny balls and lay them on the plate. Refrigerate for 20 minutes.

Suggestion for Serving: Serve cold and enjoy. Add 12 teaspoon of ground ginger as a variation. Per Serving Nutritional Values:

54 calories | 2 g fat | 32 mg sodium | 9 g carbs | 1.9 g fiber | 5.5 g sugar | 1 g protein

Chicken Caprese Sandwich

Time to prepare: 10 minutes

Time to Cook: 6 minutes

4 servings Ingredients:

- 4 tablespoons extra virgin olive oil
- 1 teaspoon of lemon juice
- a quarter cup of basil leaves
- 1 teaspoon minced fresh parsley salt
- to taste, kosher
- 2 boneless chicken breasts, peeled and cut into bite-size chunks
- to taste add black pepper
- 8 sourdough bread pieces
- 11 tomatoes with Campari
- 8 ounces mozzarella cheese, as needed, sliced balsamic vinegar

Preparation:

1. In a mixing dish, combine the chicken pieces, olive oil, lemon juice, salt, parsley, and pepper.

2. Toss the chicken in the mixture until it is uniformly coated. Remove from the equation.

3. In a medium-sized skillet, heat some oil. Cook for six minutes on each sides after adding the chicken.

4. Drizzle olive oil on the bread pieces and toast them in the oven.

5. Top each slice of bread with the chicken, cheese, and tomato slices.

6. Toss the bread pieces with the vinegar, oil, salt, basil, and pepper and serve.

Serve with basil leaves as a garnish.

Use crusty ciabatta instead of sourdough bread as a variation.

Per Serving Nutritional Values:

612.73 calories | 32.06 g fat | 891 mg sodium | 46.5 g carbs | 2.2 g fiber | 2.4 g sugar | 34.4 g protein

Peanut Butter Balls
10 minute prep time

Time to prepare: 10 minutes

16 servings Ingredients:

- 1/4 cup unsweetened shredded coconut

- 2 cups rolled oats

- a quarter cup of chocolate chips

- 12 c. honey

- a pound of peanut butter

Directions:

1. In a mixing basin, add the oats and other ingredients and stir until thoroughly incorporated.

2. Form tiny balls out of the oats mixture and lay on the plate, then chill for 15 minutes.

Suggestion for Serving: Serve cold and enjoy. Other nut butters may also be used as a variation. Per Serving Nutritional Values:

191 calories | 10.6 g fat | 78 mg sodium | 20.8 g carbs | 2.4 g fiber | 11.8 g sugar | 5.7 g protein

Veggie Tortilla Wraps
Time to Prepare: 20 minutes

Time to prepare: 5 minutes

6 servings indgredients

- 1/2 finely sliced tiny zucchini

- 1/2 teaspoon extra virgin olive oil

- 1/2 seeded and thinly sliced medium red bell pepper

- 2 tortillas (whole-grain)

- 1/2 cup baby spinach, fresh 1 teaspoon oregano, dry

- 1/4 cup hummus

- 1 finely sliced red onion

- 2 tablespoons crumbled feta cheese

- 1 tablespoon pitted and sliced black olives

Preparation:

1. In a small pan over medium-low heat, heat the olive oil. Combine the bell pepper, zucchini, and onion in a mixing bowl.

2. Cook for roughly 5 minutes on medium heat.

3. In a separate skillet, warm the tortillas one at a time until they are warm.

4. Spread hummus equally over the center of each wrap.

5. Toss the spinach with the sautéed veggies, feta cheese, oregano, and olives on each tortilla.

6. Carefully fold the tortilla's sides over the contents and roll it up.

7. Serve each roll by slicing it in half crosswise.

Serve with a nutritious dip of your choosing as a side dish.

Corn tortillas may also be used as a variation.

Per Serving Nutritional Values:

282 calories | 10.4 g fat | 3.6 g saturated fat | 39.2 g carbohydrates | 8.4 g fiber | 6.8 g sugar | 10.4 g protein

Chickpea Spinach Patties

Time to prepare: 10 minutes

Time to Cook:: 10 minutes

6 Servings Ingredients:

- 1 egg
- 2 cups washed and drained chickpeas
- 1 teaspoon cumin powder
- paprika (1 tablespoon)
- 12 onion, chopped
- 1 carrot, grated
- 1 teaspoon garlic, minced
- 1 cup cooked and drained baby spinach
- Pepper
- Salt

Directions:

1. Place chickpeas in a mixing basin and mash them with a fork.

2. Toss in the other ingredients and stir until fully blended.

115

3. Coat a pan with cooking spray and heat on medium-high.

4. Form patties from the chickpea mixture and fry for 4-5 minutes on each side or until golden brown in a hot pan.

Serving Suggestion: Serve with a dip of your choice.

Add 14 cup chopped scallions as a variation.

Per Serving Nutritional Values:

60 calories | 1 gram of fat | 143 milligrams of sodium | 10.6 grams of carbohydrates | 2.3 grams of fiber | 0.5 milligrams of sugar | 2.7 grams of protein

Crispy Chickpeas

Time to Prepare: 10 minutes

Time to cook: 4 minutes

6 people servings ingredients:

- 30 ounces washed chickpeas in a can

- 2 tbsp all-purpose bagel seasoning

- 3 tablespoons extra virgin olive oil

Directions:

1. Preheat the oven to 400 degrees Fahrenheit.

2. Toss chickpeas with oil in a mixing dish, then lay out on a baking sheet and roast for 30 minutes in a preheated oven. Halfway through, stir everything together.

3. Toss chickpeas with bagel seasoning in a large mixing basin.

Allow time for the dish to cool fully before serving.

Seasonings of your choosing may be added as a variation.

Per Serving Nutritional Values:

238 calories | 1.2 g fat | 439 mg sodium | 33.9 g carbs | 6.4 g fiber | 0.2 g sugar | 7.3 g protein

Cauliflower Fritters

Time to prepare: 10 minutes

Time to Cook: 50 minutes

4 servings Ingredients:

- 30 ounces washed and drained canned chickpeas

- 2.1/2 tablespoons extra virgin olive oil

- 2 cups cauliflower florets, chopped

- 1 small yellow onion

- 2 teaspoons minced garlic

- a sprinkle of black pepper and a pinch of salt

Preparation:

1. Spread half of the chickpeas on a parchment-lined baking sheet, drizzle with 1 tablespoon of oil, season with salt and pepper, stir, and bake for 30 minutes at 400°F.

2. Place the baked chickpeas in a food processor and pulse until smooth. Transfer the mixture to a bowl.

3. Heat /12 tbsp oil in a pan over medium-high heat, then add the garlic and onion and cook for 3 minutes.

4. Add the cauliflower and continue to simmer for another 6 minutes. Transfer the mixture to a blender, along with the remaining uncooked chickpeas, and process until smooth.

5. Pour the blended mixture on top of the fried chickpeas. After stirring the ingredients, form it into medium fritters.

6. Heat the remaining oil in a pan over medium-high heat. Cook the fritters for 3 minutes on each side before serving.

Garnish with parsley before serving.

Use fresh cauliflower instead than frozen since frozen cauliflower has more moisture, making the fritters mushy.

Per Serving Nutritional Values:

333 calories | 12.6 g fat | 65 mg sodium | 44.7 g carbs | 12.8 g fiber | 21.5 g sugar | 13.6 g protein

Salmon and Celery Salad Wraps

Time to Prepare: 10 minutes

Time to cook: 0 minutes

4 servings Ingredients:

- 1 pound cooked and flaked salmon fillet
- 1 diced carrot
- 1 diced celery stalk
- 1 small red onion, diced
- 3 tablespoons fresh dill, chopped capers,
- 2 tablespoons
- 1.1/2 tbsp extra-virgin extra-virgin olive oil
- 1 tablespoon balsamic vinegar, aged
- to taste add sea salt and black pepper
- 4 tortillas (whole-wheat)

Preparation:

1. In a large mixing bowl, combine the salmon, carrots, celery, dill, red onion, capers, oil, vinegar, pepper, and salt.

2. Toss the salmon salad with the flatbreads and serve.

3. Fold the tortillas in half, then wrap them up and serve.

Garnish with chopped cilantro before serving. Tortillas may be replaced with whole-wheat flatbread as a variation. Per Serving Nutritional Values:

336 calories | 16 g fat | 628 mg sodium | 23 g carbs | 2.8 g fiber | 2.5 g sugar | 20.3 g protein

Lamb-Filled Pita with Yogurt Sauce

15-minute prep time

Time to cook: 6 minutes

4 servings Ingredients:

- 1 tablespoon minced fresh rosemary

- 2 minced garlic cloves

- To taste, season with salt and black pepper.

- 2 teaspoons extra virgin olive oil

- 3/4 pound boneless leg of lamb, cut into bite-sized pieces

- 1.1/2 cup cucumber, finely chopped

- 4 (6-ounce) whole-wheat pitas, warmed

- 1 fat-free, plain Greek yogurt container (6 oz.)

- 1 tablespoon lemon juice, freshly squeezed

Preparation:

1. In a mixing dish, combine the rosemary, garlic, salt, and black pepper.

2. Toss in the lamb pieces and toss well to coat.

3. In a nonstick skillet, heat the olive oil over medium-high heat.

4. Transfer the lamb mixture to the skillet and cook for approximately 6 minutes, stirring occasionally.

5. For the yogurt sauce, combine the cucumber, yogurt, lemon juice, salt, and black pepper in a bowl.

6. Distribute the lamb mixture equally among all of the pitas.

7. Drizzle the yogurt sauce all over the lamb and serve right away.

Serving Suggestion: Before serving, sprinkle with mint leaves.

Plain yogurt can be substituted for Greek yogurt in this recipe.

Per Serving Nutritional Values:

675 calories | 14.1 g fat | 4 g saturated fat | 97.8 g carbohydrates | 13.2 g fiber | 3.9 g sugar | 45.3 g protein

Easy Toasted Almonds

Time to Prepare: 10 minutes

Time to Cook: 10 minutes

2 cup servings Ingredients:

- 1 tablespoon extra-virgin olive oils
- 1 teaspoon salts
- 2 cups skin-on raw whole almonds

Preparation:

1. In a 12-inch nonstick frying pan, heat the oil over moderate to high heat until it just begins to shimmer.

2. Add the almonds, salt, and pepper and turn the heat down to medium-low.

3. Cook, stirring regularly, for about 8 minutes, or until the almonds become fragrant and their color darkens somewhat.

4. Transfer the almonds to a platter lined with paper towels to cool completely before serving.

Serve over ice cream as a dessert option. Variation Tip: For a hotter outcome, add chili. Per Serving Nutritional Values:

230 calories | 22 grams of fat | 1163 milligrams of sodium | 6 grams of carbohydrates | 4 grams of fiber | 1 gram of sugar | 6 grams of protein

Parsley Nachos

Time to Prepare: 10 minutes

Time to cook: 0 minutes

3 servings Ingredients:

- tortilla chips, 3 oz.
- a quarter-cup of Greek yogurt
- 14 teaspoon garlic, minced
- 1 tablespoon fresh parsley, chopped
- 2 kalamata olives, chopped paprika,
- 1 teaspoon
- 1/4 teaspoon thyme powder

Preparation:

1. In a mixing bowl, combine all of the ingredients except the tortilla chips.

2. Gently combine the tortilla chips with the rest of the ingredients.

3. Serve right away.

Garnish with fresh chopped parsley before serving.

If extra paprika is required, add it now.

Per Serving Nutritional Values:

81 calories | 1.6 g fat | 39 mg sodium | 14.1 g carbs | 2.2 g fiber | 0.3 g sugar | 3.5 g protein

Zucchini Chips

Time to prepare: 10 minutes;

time to cook: 12 minutes; number of servings: 4

Ingredients:

- 1 thinly sliced zucchini
- a smidgeon of salt
- To taste, black pepper
- 1 tsp thyme (dried)
- a single egg
- 1 teaspoon powdered garlic
- 1 pound of almond flour

Preparation:

1. Preheat the oven to 450 degrees Fahrenheit.

2. Whisk the egg with a pinch of salt in a mixing bowl.

3. In a separate bowl, combine the flour, thyme, black pepper, and garlic powder.

4. After dredging the zucchini slices in the egg mixture, coat them with flour.

5. Place the chips on a baking sheet coated with parchment paper and bake for 6 minutes on each side.

6. Serve and have fun.

Serve with your favorite dip as a side dish. Optional Seasoning: Feel free to add extra seasoning if desired. Per Serving Nutritional Values:

67 calories | 8.2 g fat | 82 mg sodium | 3.9 g carbs | 1.5 g fiber | 1.4 g sugar | 3.6 g protein

Butternu Squash Fries

Time to Prepare: 10 minutes

Time to prepare: 20 minutes

- 6 Servings Ingredients:

- 1 seeded butternut squash

- 1 tbsp extra-virgin extra-virgin olive oil

- 12 tblsp grape seed oil to taste with sea salt

Preparation:

1. Preheat the oven to 425 degrees Fahrenheit.

2. Thinly slice the squash and arrange the pieces in a basin.

3. Drizzle the extra-virgin olive oil and grapeseed oil over the slices.

4. Toss in a pinch of salt and toss well to coat.

5. Arrange the squash slices on three baking trays and bake for 20 minutes, tossing halfway during the cooking time.

Serving Suggestion: Serve with a sauce of your choice.

Add 12 teaspoon paprika and 12 teaspoon dry thyme for a different taste.

Per Serving Nutritional Values:

153 calories | 10 g fat | 123 mg sodium | 10 g carbs | 16.4 g fiber | 2.8 g sugar | 1.5 g protein

Cauliflower Curry

Time to prepare: 10 minutes

Time to Cook: 25 minutes

4 servings Ingredients:

- 2 tablespoons olive oil

- 12 cauliflower florets, chopped

- a quarter teaspoon of salt

- 1 tablespoon curry powder

- 1 cup coconut milk (unsweetened)

- ¼ cup fresh cilantro, chopped

- 1 tablespoon lime juice

Preparation:

1. Sauté the cauliflower for 10 minutes in heated olive oil over medium heat.

2. Combine the coconut milk and curry powder in a mixing bowl, then pour over the cauliflower and cook for ten minutes.

3. Toss in the lime juice and cilantro until fully combined.

4. Finally, serve and enjoy!

Variation Tip: For a more vivid flavor, use black pepper. Garnish with chives and serve over hot rice as a side dish.

Per Serving Nutritional Values:

243 calories | 24 grams of fat | 179 milligrams of sodium | 9 grams of carbohydrates | 2 grams of fiber | 3.9 milligrams of sugar| 3 grams of protein.

Spicy Zucchini

Time to prepare: 10 minutes

Time to Cook: 5 minutes

4 servings Ingredients:

- 4 zucchini, sliced into 1/2-inch chunks
- 1 quart of water
- 1/2 teaspoon seasoning (Italian)
- 1/2 teaspoon crushed red pepper
- 1 teaspoon minced garlic
- 1 tablespoon extra virgin olive oil
- 12 cannon tomatoes, crumbled
- season with salt to taste

Preparation:

1. Fill an Instant Pot halfway with water and zucchini.

2. Cover the saucepan with the cover and cook for 2 minutes on high.

3. When you're finished, use fast release to relieve the strain. Take off the cover.

4. Clean the Instant Pot after draining the zucchini.

5. Set the Instant Pot to Sauté mode and add the oil.

6. Cook for 30 seconds after adding the garlic.

7. Stir in the remaining ingredients well. Cook for a total of 2–3 minutes.

8. Finally, serve and enjoy.

Serve over rice as a side dish. Variation Tip: For a spicier meal, add chili. Per Serving Nutritional Values:

69 calories | 4.1 g fat | 95 mg sodium | 7.9 g carbs | 2.7 g fiber | 3.5 g sugar | 2.7 g protein

Balsamic Roasted Green Beans

Time to prepare: 10 minutes

Time to Cook: 17 minutes

1 cup of servings Ingredients:

- green beans, 1 pound

- 2 chopped garlic cloves

- 1 tblsp balsamic vinaigrette

- 1 tablespoon extra virgin olive oil

- 1/8 teaspoon of salt

- 1/8 teaspoon of pepper

Preparation:

1. Preheat the oven to 425 degrees Fahrenheit.

2. In a large mixing bowl, combine the green beans, olive oil, pepper, and salt.

3. Arrange the green beans on a baking sheet coated with foil or parchment paper in an even layer.

4. Bake for 10–12 minutes, or until the beans are light brown in color.

5. Toss the green beans with the garlic and toss well to incorporate.

6. Return the beans to the oven for another 5 minutes.

7. Take the pan out of the oven and drizzle with balsamic vinegar.

Garnish with pine nuts before serving.

For a unique touch, use lemon-flavored balsamic vinegar.

Per Serving Nutritional Values:

93 calories | 5 grams of fat | 1227 milligrams of sodium | 12 grams of carbohydrates | 4 grams of fiber | 3.2 milligrams of sugar | 4 grams of protein

Mediterranean Sautéed Kale

Time to prepare: 10 minutes

Time toCook: 10 minutes

6 servings ingredients:

- 12 cups chopped kale

- lemon juice (two teaspoons)

- 1 tablespoon extra virgin olive oil

- 1 tablespoon minced garlic

- a tablespoon of soy sauce

- To taste, season with salt and black pepper.

Preparation:

1. In a saucepan, place a steamer insert.

2. Fill the saucepan with water until the steamer insert is submerged.

3. Bring the water to a boil, covered, over medium-high heat.

4. Steam the kale for 7–8 minutes in the steamer insert.

5. In a large mixing bowl, combine the lemon juice, olive oil, garlic, salt, soy sauce, and black pepper. Mix thoroughly.

6. Toss in the kale that has been steamed, and serve.

Serve the kale on its own or in a grain bowl as a side dish.

Add chile for a spicy variation.

Per Serving Nutritional Values:

91 calories | 4 g fat | 109 mg sodium | 14 g carbs | 2.1 g fiber | 0.1 g sugar | 5 g protein

Green Bean Stew

Time to prepare: 10 minutes

Time to Cook: 40 minutes

4 servings Ingredients:

- 1/4 cup extra-virgin extra- 3 sliced garlic cloves
- 1 diced sweet onion,
- Season with sea salt and crushed black pepper
- 1 pound fresh green beans, cut into 2-inch chunks with the ends clipped
- 1 tomato sauce can (8 oz.)
- 1/2 cup of water

Preparation:

1. Place the olive oil in a small pan over medium heat and let it to heat up.

2. Add the onion and garlic and cook for 3 minutes, or until the garlic is aromatic.

3. Add salt and pepper to taste.

4. Gently toss the beans into the pan with a spoon; cover and simmer for 10 minutes.

5. Add the tomato sauce and water and mix well.

6. Cover and cook for another 25 minutes.

7. Finally, serve and enjoy!

Garnish with freshly cut parsley and serve over rice as a side dish. Use three big peeled tomatoes instead of the canned tomatoes as a variation. Per Serving Nutritional Values:

159 calories | 13 g fat | 306 mg sodium | 12 g carbs | 5.4 g fiber | 5.2 g sugar | 3 g protein

Cauliflower and Carrot Stir Fry

Time to prepare: 10 minutes

Time to Cook: 10 minutes

4 servings Ingredients:

- 12 teaspoon ground cumin
- 3 tablespoons olive oil
- 1 big onion, chopped
- 1 tablespoon garlic, minced
- 2 cups carrots, diced
- 4 cups cauliflower florets, washed

Preparation:

1. Heat the olive oil in a large frying pan over medium heat.

2. Cook for 3 minutes after adding the onion, garlic, and carrots.

3. Chop the cauliflower into 1-inch pieces or bite-size chunks.

4. Toss the cauliflower, salt, and cumin into the carrots and onions in the pan to mix. Cook for 3 minutes with the lid on.

5. Continue to cook for 3–4 minutes more, uncovered.

6. Serve immediately.

Serve with flatbread or rice as a side dish.

Make sure to slice the cauliflower into tiny florets as a variation tip.

Per Serving Nutritional Values:

159 calories | 0.2 g fat | 70 mg sodium | 15 g carbs | 4.7 g fiber | 6.7 g sugar | 3 g protein

Mushroom and Tomato Bake

Time to prepare: 10 minutes

Time to Cook 20 minutes

6 servings Ingredients

- 2 pound mushrooms, cleaned and blotted dry
- 1 quart of red wine
- 1/2 cup extra-virgin extra-virgin olive oil
- 1/4 teaspoon salt
- 3 tomatoes, cut
- 1 teaspoon oregano, dry

Preparation:

1. Preheat the oven to 400 degrees Fahrenheit.

2. Arrange the mushrooms on a baking sheet.

3. Drizzle with olive oil and season with oregano, wine, and salt. After mixing well, bake for about 20 minutes.

4. Season with salt and pepper.

5. Serve.

Serve with steak, chicken, or pork as a side dish.

Add any additional dry herbs you choose as a variation.

Per Serving Nutritional Values:

156 calories | 18 grams of fat | 220 milligrams of sodium | 14 grams of carbohydrates | 2.4 grams of fiber | 4.5 grams of sugar | 6 grams of protein

Mediterranean Gnocchi

Time to prepare: 5 minutes

Time to cook: 2 minutes

- 6 servings Ingredients:
- 1 cup chopped chargrilled veggies
- 2 gnocchi cups
- 2 tablespoons pesto (red)
- One forth cup of Pecorino cheese
- 12 cup basil flowers

Preparation:

1. Bring a large saucepan of water to a boil, season with salt, and add the gnocchi.

2. Cook the gnocchi for 2 minutes before draining them thoroughly.

3. Add a splash of water to the gnocchi and return to the pot.

4. Combine the chargrilled veggies, basil leaves, and red pesto in a large mixing bowl.

5. Sprinkle with Pecorino and serve right away.

Serve with a side salad as a side dish.

Pecorino cheese may be substituted with parmesan cheese as a variation.

Per Serving Nutritional Values:

398 calories | 12.2 g fat | 2 g saturated fat | 56.4 g carbohydrates | 1.1 g fiber | 0 g sugar | 12.7 g protein

Stewed Okra

Time to prepare: 10 minutes

Time to Cook: 25 minutes

4 servings Ingredients:

- 4 garlic cloves, finely chopped

- 1 pound cleaned fresh or frozen okra 1 can (15 oz.) basic tomato sauce 2 c. liquid

- 1/4 cup extra virgin olive oil 1 sliced onion

- 1/2 cup coarsely chopped fresh cilantro

Preparation:

1. Heat the olive oil, onion, garlic, and salt in a large saucepan over medium heat. Cook, stirring occasionally, until the onion has softened and the garlic has become aromatic.

2. Cook for 3 minutes after adding the okra.

3. Combine the tomato sauce, water, cilantro, and black pepper in a large mixing bowl; whisk to combine, cover, and simmer for 15 minutes, stirring regularly.

4. Serve immediately.

Serve over rice as a side dish.

Replace the tinned tomatoes with two fresh, peeled tomatoes as a variation.

Per Serving Nutritional Values:

201 calories | 12.9 grams of fat | 43 milligrams of sodium |
18 grams of carbohydrates | 5.8 grams of fiber | 7.3
milligrams of sugar | 4 grams of protein

Roasted Vegetables

Time to Prepare: 10 minutes

15 minutes to cook

4 servings Ingredients:

- 1 zucchini, finely chopped
- 1/2 teaspoon oregano, dry
- a quarter teaspoon of garlic powder basil (1 teaspoon)
- 1/2 tblsp parsley
- 2 tablespoons extra virgin olive oil
- 2 chopped tiny onions
- a ten grape tomato
- 3 sliced bell peppers
- a quarter teaspoon of salt

Directions:

1. Preheat the oven to 425 degrees Fahrenheit.

2. Combine all ingredients in a mixing basin and toss to combine.

3. Arrange the veggies on a baking sheet and roast for 15 minutes in a preheated oven. Halfway through, stir everything together.

Allow time for the dish to cool fully before serving.

Seasonings of your choosing may be added as a variation.

Per Serving Nutritional Values:

168 calories | 8 g fat | 314 mg sodium | 24 g carbs | 6.3 g fiber | 15 g sugar | 4.7 g protein

Chickpeas with Veggies

Time to Prepare: 10 minutes

7-minute cook time

2 servings ingredients

- 2 cups washed and drained chickpeas

- 1/4 cup basil leaves, chopped

- 1 teaspoon seeds of Nigella sativa,

- 1 tblsp of sesame seeds

- 1 tablespoon extra virgin olive oil

- 1 teaspoon minced garlic

- 1 teaspoon chili powder

- 1 sliced bell pepper

- 1 chopped small onion

- 1 zucchini, finely chopped

- 4 chopped medium tomatoes

Directions:

1. In a large pan, combine the onion and tomatoes and cook for 3-4 minutes over medium-high heat.

2. Stir in the chickpeas, cover, and cook for 5 minutes.

3. Stir in the bell peppers, zucchini, and garlic for 2 minutes.

4. Remove the pan from the heat. Combine the oil and basil in a bowl.

5. Add Nigella seeds, chili powder, and sesame seeds to the mix.

Serving Suggestion: Combine all ingredients in a large mixing bowl and stir thoroughly. Serve immediately. 14 teaspoon paprika may be added as a variation. Per Serving Nutritional Values:

487 calories | 15.5 g fat | 752 mg sodium | 75.9 g carbs | 16.8 g fiber | 12.1 g sugar | 16.9 g protein

Vegetarian Chili

Time to prepare: 2 minutes

30 minutes to cook

2 servings : Ingredients:

- 1/4 ounces oven-roasted veggies

- 1 tomato can (chopped)

- 1 can chili-flavored kidney beans

- To taste, season with salt and black pepper.

Preparation:

1. Lightly butter a casserole dish and preheat the oven to 390°F.

2. Arrange the veggies in a casserole dish and bake for 30 minutes.

3. Bake for approximately 15 minutes and then toss in the kidney beans, tomatoes, salt, and black pepper.

4. Bake for another 15 minutes.

5. Take the dish out of the oven and serve.

Serve with ready-made mixed grains as a side dish. You may use navy beans instead of kidney beans as a variation. Per Serving Nutritional Values:

366 calories | 15 grams of fat | 2.5 grams of saturated fat | 43.8 grams of carbohydrates | 15.4 grams of fiber | 8.5 grams of sugar | 14.4 grams of protein

Tabbouleh

Prep Time: 20 minutes

Serves: 3 Ingredients:

- 3 tablespoons olive oil, divided
- ½ cup bulgur, uncooked
- 2 cups boiling vegetable broth
- 3 cups fresh Italian flat-leaf parsley, chopped
- ¼ cup scallions, chopped
- ½ teaspoon salt
- 3 fresh Roma tomatoes, cored and chopped
- ½ cup fresh mint, chopped
- 2 tablespoons fresh lemon juice

Preparation:

1.   In a large bowl, mix the bulgur thoroughly with 1 tablespoon of the olive oil.

2.   Pour in the hot vegetable broth and cover the bowl tightly with plastic wrap.

3.   Set aside for about 1 hour until the bulgur has softened.

4.   Strain the bulgur through a fine-mesh strainer.

5.   In a large serving bowl, mix the bulgur and 2 tablespoons of olive oil and the rest of the ingredients until well combined.

6.   Serve immediately.

Serving Suggestion: Serve with grilled vegetables. Variation Tip: Scallions can be replaced with red onions. Nutritional Information per Serving:

Calories: 244 | Fat: 14.8g | Sat Fat: 2.2g | Carbohydrates: 26.6g | Fiber: 7.7g | Sugar: 5.1g | Protein: 4.7g

Garlicky Mashed Cauliflower

Time to Prepare: 10 minutes

Time to cook: 3 hours on high

6 servings Ingredients:

- 1 cauliflower head, sliced into florets

- 1 peeled little head of garlic

- 4 cups. of vegetable stock

- a third of a cup of sour cream

- 4 tablespoons chopped fresh herbs: chives, parsley, and spring onions

- To taste, season with salt and black pepper.

Preparation:

1. In a slow cooker, combine the cauliflower and garlic. Pour the liquid over the cauliflower until it is completely coated. If necessary, add extra liquid.

2. Cover and cook on high for 3 hours.

3. Drain the liquid and save it aside for later use.

4. Using a fork or a potato masher, mash the veggies.

5. Return to step 5 and mash until smooth.

6. To soften the mash, add part of the saved cooking liquid.

7. Add the chopped herbs and season with salt and freshly ground pepper. Stir everything together completely.

Serve heated with roast chicken as a side dish.

Switch out the veggie broth with chicken broth as a variation.

Per Serving Nutritional Values:

83 calories | 3.8 g fat | 531 mg sodium | 7.8 g carbs | 1.7 g fiber | 1.7 g sugar | 13 g protein

Roasted Carrots

Time to prepare: 10 minutes

Time to cook: 20 minutes

4 servings Ingredients:

- 1.1/2 pound carrots (peeled and sliced)
- 1/2 cup crumbled Feta cheese
- 1 garlic clove, minced
- 2 tablespoons dill, chopped
- 2 tablespoons extra virgin olive oil
- 1 teaspoon distilled water
- honey (two tablespoons)
- Pepper
- Salt

Directions:

1. Preheat the oven to 425 degrees Fahrenheit.

2. Arrange carrots in a single layer on the baking sheet.

3. Toss carrots in a mixture of honey, water, oil, garlic, dill, pepper, and salt.

4. Roast for 20-25 minutes in a preheated oven. Halfway through, stir everything together.

Serve with a sprinkling of Feta cheese on top. Add 2 tablespoons chopped basil as a variation. Per Serving Nutritional Values:

216 calories | 11.1 g fat | 369 mg sodium | 27.3 g carbs | 4.4 g fiber | 17.8 g sugar | 4.4 g protein

Ratatouille

Time to prepare: 10 minutes

Time to prepare: 40 minutes

8 servings Ingredients:

Veggies

- 2 sliced zucchinis
- 2 sliced eggplants
- 2 sliced yellow squashes
- 6 sliced Roma tomatoes

Sauce

- 2 tablespoon olive oil
- 1 onion, chopped
- 4 garlic cloves, minced
- 1 diced red bell pepper
- 1 diced yellow bell pepper
- 28 ounces crushed tomatoes
- 2 tablespoons fresh basil, chopped
- salt and pepper to taste

seasoning with herbs

- 1 teaspoon garlic, minced

- 2 tablespoons fresh basil, chopped

- 2 teaspoons chopped fresh parsley

- thyme, 2 tblsp.

- Season with salt and pepper to taste.

- 4 tablespoons extra virgin olive oil

Preparation:

1. Preheat the oven to 375 degrees Fahrenheit.

2. In an oven-safe pan, heat the olive oil. For approximately 10 minutes, sauté the onion, garlic, and bell peppers.

3. Add the smashed tomatoes and season with salt and pepper. Mix thoroughly.

4. Remove the pan from the heat and add 2 tablespoons basil leaves, chopped. Stir until the mixture is completely smooth.

5. Arrange the sliced vegetables on top of the sauce, seasoning with salt and pepper as needed.

6. Combine basil, parsley, thyme, garlic, salt, pepper, and olive oil in a large mixing bowl. Season the veggies with this herb seasoning.

7. Place the pan in the oven and bake for 40 minutes, covered with foil.

8. Remove the cover and continue baking for another 20 minutes, or until the veggies are softened.

9. Serve!

Serve with seared flank steak as a side dish.

Cut the vegetables into pieces or slices for a different look.

Per Serving Nutritional Values:

230 calories | 11 g fat | 1112 mg sodium | 32 g carbs | 8 g fiber | 6 g sugar | 5 g protein

Vegetable Curry
Time to Prepare: 20 minutes
30 minutes to cooking time
6 servings ingredients

- 6 tablespoons olive oil, split

- 2 peeled and sliced carrots

- 1 peeled and sliced sweet potato

- 1 chopped onion

- 1 seeded and sliced red bell pepper curry powder (about 1 tablespoon)

- 1 teaspoon cinnamon powder

- a quarter teaspoon of salt

- 1 sliced zucchini

- 1/4 cup blanched almonds

- 10 ounces fresh spinach

- 1 medium cubed eggplant

- 1 seeded and sliced green bell pepper

- 3 minced garlic cloves

- 1 teaspoon turmeric powder

- 3/4 teaspoon cayenne pepper, ground

- 1 cup fresh orange juice 1 15-ounce can low-sodium garbanzo beans, washed and drained

- 2 tablespoons raisins (golden)

Preparation:

3. Heat 3 tablespoons olive oil in a large wok over medium-high heat.

2. Cook for 5 minutes with the sweet potato, carrots, eggplant, onion, and bell peppers.

3. Meanwhile, heat the remaining olive oil in a separate frying pan over medium heat.

4. Saute for 3 minutes with the garlic, cinnamon, curry powder, turmeric, salt, and cayenne pepper.

5. Add the garlic mixture to the veggies in the pan and stir well to incorporate.

6. Combine the zucchini, beans, orange juice, raisins, and almonds in a large mixing bowl.

7. Simmer for around 20 minutes with the lid on the pan.

8. Take off the cover and add the spinach.

9. Remove the cover and cook for another 5 minutes before serving.

Serve over a bed of rice as a side dish.

Almonds may be used instead of cashews as a variation.

Per Serving Nutritional Values:

517 calories | 21.1 grams of fat | 2.7 grams of saturated fat | 70.1 grams of carbohydrates | 19.8 grams of fiber | 21.2 grams of sugar | 18.8 grams of protein

Turkish Beet Greens

Time to Prepare: 10 minutes

Time to Cook: 10 minutes

2 servings Ingredients:

- 2 cups green beets
- 7 stemmed and quartered dried Turkish figs
- 1/2 cup white vineyard juice
- 2 cups spinach (fresh)
- 1 garlic clove, minced
- 2 teaspoons extra virgin olive oil
- season with salt to taste
- 1/2 oz. grated parmesan cheese (optional)

Preparation:

1. In a skillet over medium heat, cook the beet greens, white grape juice, and figs for approximately seven minutes before adding the olive oil, spinach, and garlic.

2. Reduce the heat to low and simmer for three more minutes before seasoning with salt.

3. Before serving, sprinkle the parmesan cheese over top.

Serve with grilled meat as a side dish.

Add some chili flakes for a kick of heat.

Per Serving Nutritional Values:

328 calories | 7 g fat | 260 mg sodium | 49.4 g carbs | 10.2 g fiber | 30 g sugar | 6.7 g protein

Zucchini and Tomato Casserole

Time to Prepare: 10 minutes

Time to Cook: 40 minutes

2 servings Ingredients:

- 1/2 cup cherry tomatoes, halved

- 4 cups zucchini, sliced

- 1 teaspoon garlic, minced

- 1 tablespoon extra virgin olive oil

- 1/2 cup grated parmesan cheese

- 1/4 cup breadcrumbs

- 4 tablespoons basil leaves

- Season with salt and pepper to taste.

Preparation:

1. Preheat the oven to 350 degrees Fahrenheit.

2. In a pan over medium heat, heat the olive oil and sauté the zucchini, salt, and pepper for 10 minutes.

3. Cook until the garlic is aromatic.

4. Combine the zucchini, tomatoes, and basil in a baking dish.

5. Sprinkle breadcrumbs and parmesan cheese over top.

6. Bake for 30 minutes at 350°F.

Garnish with fresh basil before serving. Feel free to use your favorite herbs as a variation. Per Serving Nutritional Values:

185 calories | 9.7 g fat | 302 mg sodium | 20.4 g carbs | 4.2 g fiber | 6.8 g sugar | 7.3 g protein

Spelt-Stuffed Peppers

Time to Prepare: 20 minutes

Time to cook: 25 minutes

4 servings Ingredients:

- 4 big red peppers, de-seeded and halved

- a cup of sundried tomatoes (12 cup)

- 2 tablespoons extra virgin olive oil

- 1 red onion spiralized using the spiralizer's flat blade

- 1 zucchini, spiralized into thin strands

- Pre-cooked spelt in a 9-ounce pouch

- 1/2 cup olives (mixed)

- 1/2 cup basil, crumbled

- To taste, season with salt and black pepper.

Preparation:

1. Preheat oven to 390°F and oil a roasting pan gently.

2. Place the red peppers cut-side up on the roasting tray and drizzle with 1 tablespoon of olive oil.

3. Season to taste with salt and pepper, then bake for 25 minutes.

4. Meanwhile, heat the remaining olive oil in a skillet over medium heat and add the spiralized onion.

5. Cook for 3 minutes, or until the vegetables are softened, then transfer to a bowl.

6. Combine the zucchini, spelt, olives, sundried tomatoes, and basil in a large mixing bowl.

7. Fill the red peppers to the brim with the mixture.

8. Roast for about 5 minutes before serving.

Serve with a green salad as a side dish.

Variation Tip: You can also use any other tomato variety.

Per Serving Nutritional Values:

412 calories | 12.5 grams of fat | 1.5 grams of saturated fat | 64.3 grams of carbohydrates | 12.4 grams of fiber | 7.6 grams of sugar | 12.2 grams of protein

Roasted Brussels Sprouts and Pecans

Time to Prepare: 10 minutes

Time to Cook: 3 hours

4 servings Ingredients:

Fresh Brussels sprouts,

- 1.1/2 pound

- 4 tablespoons extra virgin olive oil

- 4 garlic cloves, minced water (three tablespoons)

- Season with salt and pepper to taste.

- 1/2 cup chopped pecans

Preparation:

1. In an Instant Pot or pressure cooker, combine all of the ingredients. Stir everything together well.

2. Make sure the steam release valve is set to vent and close the lid.

3. Cook on low for 3 hours.

4. Finish with a squeeze of lemon juice.

Serve with grilled meat as a side dish.

Pecans may be replaced with chestnuts or walnuts as a variation.

Per Serving Nutritional Values:

161 calories | 13.1 g fat | 43 mg sodium | 10.2 g carbs | 6.8 g fiber | 3.8 g sugar | 4.1 g protein

White Beans with Tomato and Arugula
Time to Prepare:10 minutes

Time to cook: 5 minutes

6 Servings Ingredients:

- Cannellini beans, 30 ounces,

- drained and rinsed 1 teaspoon thyme, dry

- 5 oz. arugula infant

- 1 tablespoon extra virgin olive oil

- 1/2 cup drained sun-dried tomatoes

- Pepper

- Salt

Directions:

1. In a medium-high-heat saucepan, heat the oil.

2. Stir in the arugula until it has wilted, approximately 3 minutes.

3. Cook for 2-3 minutes with the thyme, beans, tomatoes, pepper, and salt.

Serving Suggestion: Combine all ingredients in a large mixing bowl and stir thoroughly. Serve warm.

Cooked spinach may be used instead of arugula as a variation.

Per Serving Nutritional Values:

133 calories | 3.5 g fat | 76 mg sodium | 19.1 g carbs | 5.7 g fiber | 0.9 g sugar | 7 g protein

Garlic Cauliflower and Zucchini

Time to Prepare: 10 minutes

Time to cook: 8 minutes

2 servings ingredients:

- 1 cup florets de cauliflower
- 12 tblsp cumin
- 1 teaspoon thyme
- 2 cloves garlic
- 1 tablespoon extra virgin olive oil
- 1 sliced bell pepper
- 1 cup sliced zucchini
- Pepper
- Salt

Directions:

1. In a medium-sized skillet, heat the oil.

2. Toss in the veggies, garlic, cumin, pepper, and salt, and mix thoroughly.

3. Cook for 3-4 minutes with the lid on.

4. Remove the top and simmer for another 2 minutes, stirring constantly. Turn off the heat in the pan.

Allow time for the dish to cool fully before serving. Drizzle with a tablespoon of fresh lemon juice as a variation. Per Serving Nutritional Values:

108 calories | 7.5 g fat | 101 mg sodium | 10.4 g carbs | 2.9 g fiber | 5.2 g sugar | 2.6 g protein

Cherry Tomatoes and Black Beans

Time to Prepare: 10 minutes

15 minutes Cooking time

2 servings ingredients:

- 1 cup cherry tomatoes,

- halved 1 (15-ounce) can black beans, undrained

- 1 teaspoon kosher salt

- 1 tablespoon oregano, dried

- 1 teaspoon crushed red pepper

Preparation:

1. In a large skillet, bring the black beans and their liquid to a low boil over medium-high heat.

2. Reduce the heat to low and continue to cook for another 5 minutes.

3. Cook for 10 minutes after adding the cherry tomatoes, salt, oregano, and red pepper flakes.

4. Finally, serve and enjoy.

Serve over hot rice as a side dish. Optional Spices: Feel free to experiment with different spices. Per Serving Nutritional Values:

Calories 185 | Fat 1g | Sodium 987mg | Carbs 34g | Fiber 12g | Sugar 2g | Protein 12g

Baked Black-Eyed Peas

15-minute prep time

Time to Cook: 35 minutes

3 servings Ingredients:

- 2 cans (15 oz.) black-eyed peas, rinsed and drained
- 3 tbsp extra-virgin olive oil
- season with salt to taste
- 2 tsp. Za'atar
- 2 tsp. sumac
- 2 tsp. harissa

Preparation:

1. Preheat the oven to 400 degrees Fahrenheit.

2. Drizzle the olive oil over the black-eyed peas on a baking sheet.

3. Season with salt and toss thoroughly to coat.

4. Bake for approximately 35 minutes, shaking the baking pan three times during the process.

5. Take the pan out of the oven and season with the Za'atar, sumac, and harissa.

6. Serve immediately.

Serving Suggestion: Serve with tea as a snack. Seasonings of your choice can be used as a variation. Per Serving Nutritional Values:

478 calories | 18.5 grams of fat | 2.3 grams of saturated fat | 66.1 grams of carbohydrates | 13.1 grams of fiber | 0.9 grams of sugar | 14.9 grams of protein

Mediterranean White Beans
Time to Prepare: 10 minutes

Time to cook: 20 minutes

4 servings Ingredients:

- 1/4 cup extra-virgin

- 1 jar (24 oz.) white beans, washed and drained

- 12 cup chopped onion

- 1 garlic clove, minced

- 1 teaspoon kosher salt

- 1 (16-ounce) can diced tomatoes, including liquid

- 12 teaspoon dry rosemary, crushed

- 12 cup celery, chopped

- 14 cup fresh Italian parsley, chopped

- 1 teaspoon sugar

Preparation:

1. In a pan over medium-high heat, heat the olive oil and sauté the garlic and onion for approximately 5 minutes.

2. Bring the white beans, tomatoes, rosemary, salt, and sugar to a boil in a large pot.

3. Lower the heat to low, cover, and cook for approximately 15 minutes.

4. Finally, add the parsley and serve.

Serving Suggestion: Serve with pork or chicken as a wonderful side dish.

Coconut milk may be used instead of almond milk as a variation.

Per Serving Nutritional Values:

346 calories | 8.3 grams of fat | 1.3 grams of saturated fat | 60.2 grams of carbohydrates | 2.1 grams of fiber | 1.8 grams of sugar | 7.9 grams of protein

Spicy Borlotti Beans

Time to Prepare: 12 hours and 10 minutes

Time to Cook: 1 hour and 50 minutes

8 servings Ingredients:

- 1 teaspoon salt, divided

- 2 tablespoons extra-virgin olive oil

- 1 pound dried borlotti beans, soaked overnight, drained, and rinsed

- 1/4 teaspoon freshly ground black pepper

- 1/4 teaspoon red pepper flakes

- 1 large onion, chopped

- 1/2 green bell pepper, seeded and chopped

- 1 (14.5-ounce) can diced tomatoes, undrained

- 3 garlic cloves, minced

- 1 (1-inch) piece fresh red chili, seeded and minced

Preparation:

1. Place the beans in a large pot with enough water to cover them and /12 teaspoon of salt.

2. Bring to a boil over medium-high heat, then reduce to a low heat and continue to cook for 1–1.1/2 hours, or until the beans are soft. Drain.

3. Heat the olive oil in a large pan over medium heat. Cook for approximately 10 minutes, or until the onion and bell pepper are softened.

4. Stir in the beans, tomatoes with their juices, garlic, chile, 1/2 teaspoon salt, black pepper, and red pepper flakes.

5. Bring to a boil, then lower to a low heat and continue to cook for another 10 minutes.

Garnish with chopped cilantro before serving. If you want a milder flavor, leave off the red chili. Per Serving Nutritional Values:

Calories 240 | Fat 4g | Sodium 335mg | Carbs 39g | Fiber 13g | Sugar 3g | Protein 13g

Black-Eyed Peas Stew
Time to Prepare: 10 minutes

Time to Cook: 55 minutes

6 Servings Ingredients

- 30 ounces black-eyed peas

- 1 yellow onion, chopped

- 1 green bell pepper, chopped

- 15 ounces tomato, diced

- 3 carrots, chopped

- 1 tablespoon lime juice

- 2 cups water

- 1.1/2 teaspoons ground cumin

- 1 bay leaf

- 1 teaspoon dried oregano

- Kosher salt, to taste

- 12 teaspoon red pepper flakes

- 12 teaspoon paprika

- Black pepper, to taste

- 1 cup fresh parsley, chopped

Preparation:

1. In a warm Dutch oven, sauté the garlic and onions in the oil for 5 minutes, stirring regularly.

2. Combine the tomatoes, pepper, water, spices, bay leaf, and salt in a large mixing bowl. Allow it to stew for a while.

3. Add the black-eyed peas and simmer for an additional 5 minutes.

4. Cover and turn down the heat. Cook for another 30 minutes.

5. Add the lime juice and stir to combine.

6. Finally, serve and enjoy.

Garnish with parsley before serving. Variation Tip: Vegetable broth may be used instead of water. Per Serving Nutritional Values:

197 calories | 6.3 g fat | 92 mg sodium | 30.4 g carbs | 7.7 g fiber | 5.4 g sugar | 8.9 g protein

Gigante Beans in Tomato Sauce

Time to Prepare: 10 minutes

Time to Cook: 5 minutes

6 Servingsmingredients

- 6 ounces tomato paste

- 1 (12-ounce) container gigante beans, undrained

- 1/2 teaspoon dried oregano

- 3/4 cup water

Preparation:

1. In a small saucepan, bring the beans and their liquid to a boil over medium-high heat.

2. Turn off the heat and drain the liquid from the pan.

3. Combine the tomato paste and water in a small saucepan and bring to a boil to cook through.

4. Place the beans on a serving platter.

5. Serve with a dollop of tomato sauce on top.

Sprinkle with the dried oregano before serving.

If you can't get gigante beans, corona beans or giant butter beans are suitable replacements.

Per Serving Nutritional Values:

238 calories | 1 gram fat | 616 milligrams sodium | 46 grams carbohydrates | 12 grams fiber | 11 grams sugar | 15 grams protein

Cannellini Beans and Farro Stew

Time to Prepare: 20 minutes

Time to prepare: 45 minutes

6 servings Ingredients:

- 1 cup peeled and sliced carrots

- 2 tablespoons extra virgin olive oil

- 4 garlic cloves, minced

- 1 cup celery, diced

- 1 cup rinsed uncooked farro

- 1 leaf of bay

- season with salt to taste

- 4 cups chopped fresh kale

- 1 tablespoon freshly squeezed lemon juice

- 1 cup chopped yellow onion

- 1 can chopped tomatoes (14.1/2 ounces)

- 1/2 cup sprigs fresh parsley

- 1 teaspoon oregano, dry

- 5 cups vegetable broth (low sodium)

- 1 can low-sodium cannellini beans (15 ounces), washed and drained

- 12 cup crumbled feta cheese

189

Preparation:

1. Heat the oil in a large skillet over medium-high heat and cook the celery, carrots, garlic, and onion for approximately 3 minutes.

2. Bring the farro, tomatoes, parsley sprigs, oregano, bay leaf, broth, and salt to a boil, stirring constantly.

3. Lower the heat to medium-low, cover, and cook for 20 minutes.

4. Remove the parsley sprigs and add the kale, simmering for 15 minutes.

5. Add the cannellini beans and simmer for 5 minutes, or until cooked through.

6. Remove the bay leaf and add the lemon juice.

7. Remove from the heat and sprinkle with feta cheese before serving.

Serve with yellow rice as a side dish. Kale may be substituted with spinach as a variation. Per Serving Nutritional Values:

520 calories | 10.5 grams of fat | 3 grams of saturated fat | 79.1 grams of carbohydrates | 22.6 grams of fiber | 6.5 grams of sugar | 30 grams of protein

Kale Fried Rice

Time to Prepare: 10 minutes

15 minutes cooking time

Serves: 2 servings Ingredients:

- 2 eggs, whisked together with some salt
- 2 tablespoons coconut oil
- ¾ cup green onions, chopped
- 2 garlic cloves, minced
- 1 cup vegetables, chopped (Brussels sprouts, carrot, bell pepper), optional
- 1 bunch kale
- ¾ cup unsweetened coconut flakes
- ¼ teaspoon sea salt
- 2 teaspoons low-sodium soy sauce
- 2 cups brown rice, cooked
- 1 lime, halved
- 2 teaspoons sriracha or chili garlic sauce
- Chopped fresh parsley, for garnish

Preparation:

1. Heat a wok over medium to high heat.

2. Add a teaspoon of oil. Coat the bottom of the wok.

3. Pour in the eggs and cook. Stir frequently. The eggs should be scrambled.

4. Transfer the eggs to a bowl. Add a teaspoon of oil to your wok.

5. Add the onions, garlic, and optional vegetables. Cook for 30 seconds.

6. Add the kale and cook for a minute more. Transfer the wok contents to the bowl of eggs. Add the remaining kale to your wok.

7. Now, pour in the coconut flakes. Cook while stirring for 30 seconds.

8. Add the rice. Cook for 3 minutes, stirring occasionally. Pour the bowl contents back into your wok.

9. Use a spoon or spatula to break up the scrambled egg.

10. Add the chili garlic sauce and the juice from the half lime. Combine well.

11. Divide the rice into serving bowls.

Serving Suggestion: Garnish with chopped parsley and lime wedges.

Variation Tip: Switch up the coconut oil with olive oil.

Per Serving Nutritional Values:

934 calories | 60 grams of fat | 260 milligrams of sodium | 154 grams of carbohydrates | 12 grams of fiber | 4 grams of sugar | 26 grams of protein

Cauliflower Rice

Time to Prepare: 10 minutes

Time to cook: 35 minutes

4 servings Ingredients:

- 1 cup grated pumpkin

- 2 cups grated cauliflower

- 4 tablespoons olive oil

- 1 small chopped white onion

- 1 teaspoon ginger paste

- 14 teaspoon turmeric powder

- 1 teaspoon curry powder

- 1 teaspoon red chili powder

- 12 cup snow peas

- 13 cup vegetable broth

- 12 cup coconut milk

Preparation:

1. Heat the olive oil in a large nonstick skillet.

2. Add the onions to the pan and cook for a few minutes.

3. Cook until the ginger is fragrant.

4. After that, add the peas and the vegetable broth. On medium heat, cover the skillet and cook for 10 minutes.

5. Remove the lid and cook for about 10 minutes with the pumpkin.

6. Pour the coconut milk into the pot.

7. Combine the curry powder, turmeric powder, and chili powder in a mixing bowl. Add the grated cauliflower next. Cook for 12 minutes with the lid on the skillet.

8. Serve immediately.

Serve with chopped green onions as a garnish. For a milder flavor, leave off the red chili powder. Per Serving Nutritional Values:

247 calories | 21.8 g fat | 95 mg sodium | 13.5 g carbs | 5.1 g fiber | 5.9 g sugar | 3.8 g protein

1. Combine the cucumbers, tomatoes, vinegar, and remaining oil in a mixing bowl, then season with salt and pepper.

2. Finally, sprinkle the cheese, parsley, and mint over the top.

Garnish with thyme sprigs before serving.

Substitute red wine vinegar for sherry vinegar as a variation.

Per Serving Nutritional Values:

359 calories | 20.9 g fat | 375 mg sodium | 36.5 g carbs | 3.2 g fiber | 3.7 g sugar | 8.9 g protein

Sweet Red Lentils

Time to Prepare: 10 minutes

15 minutes to cook

4 people Ingredients:

To make the sauce, combine the following ingredients.

- 2 cups water

- 2 tablespoons brown sugar

- 1/4 cup coconut aminos

- 2 sliced garlic cloves

- 1/2 teaspoon crushed red pepper

- 1 tablespoon fresh ginger, minced

For the lentils, prepare as follows:

- 1 tablespoon olive oil

- 1/2 diced yellow onion

- 1 cup red lentils

- 2 sliced green onions for serving

Preparation:

1. Combine all of the sauce ingredients in a jar.

2. In a large saucepan over medium-high heat, pour the oil.

3. Stir in the onion and cook for 3 minutes.

4. Once the onion has started to brown and soften, add the sauce and lentils and bring to a low boil. Simmer for 8–10 minutes with the lid on.

5. Wait until the lentils are soft and the liquid has been absorbed before continuing (mostly).

6. Serve immediately.

Garnish with parsley and green onions before serving.

For a milder flavor, leave off the crushed red pepper.

Per Serving Nutritional Values:

277 calories | 7.7 grams of fat | 27 milligrams of sodium | 39.7 grams of carbohydrates | 15.4 grams of fiber | 6.2 milligrams of sugar | 12.9 grams of protein

Kidney Beans Meal

Time to prepare: 10 minutes

Time to prepare: 0 minutes

6 servings Ingredients

1 can (15 ounces) drained and rinsed kidney beans

1/2 English chopped cucumber,

1 medium chopped heirloom tomato,

1 bunch fresh cilantro, stems removed and chopped

1 chopped red onion,

1 big lime

3 tablespoons extra-virgin olive oil

1 teaspoon mustard (Dijon)

1/2 teaspoon garlic paste (fresh)

1 tsp sumac powder

Season with salt and pepper to taste.

Preparation:

1. Combine the kidney beans, chopped vegetables, and cilantro in a medium-sized mixing basin.

2. To prepare the vinaigrette, whisk together the lime juice, oil, garlic paste, pepper, mustard, and sumac in a small basin.

3. Drizzle the vinaigrette over the salad and toss gently.

4. Season with salt and pepper. Allow for a half-hour chilling period after covering the bowl.

5. Finally, serve and enjoy!

Drizzle with balsamic vinegar as a finishing touch. Garbanzo, white, or black beans may be used as a variation. Per Serving Nutritional Values:

74 calories | 0.7 g fat | 313 mg sodium | 16 g carbs | 5.8 g fiber | 3.6 g sugar | 5.5 g protein

Barley Pilaf

Time to Prepare: 10 minutes

Time to Cook: 45 minutes

5 servings Ingredients:

- 1 small onion, coarsely chopped
- 1/4 cup fresh parsley
- 1.12 cup pearl barley, washed
- 1.12 tablespoons lemon juice
- 2 tablespoons fresh chives, minced
- 1.12 teaspoons fresh thyme, minced
- 2.1/2 garlic cloves, minced
- 3 tbsp extra-virgin extra-virgin olive oil
- 2.1/2 cups of water
- Season with salt and pepper to taste.

Preparation:

1. In a large saucepan, heat the oil over medium heat until it begins to shimmer.

2. Add the onion and 1/2 teaspoon of salt and simmer until the onion is soft (approximately 5 minutes).

3. Combine the barley, garlic, and thyme in a saucepan and simmer, turning often, until the barley is gently toasted and fragrant (approximately 3 minutes).

4. Add the water and bring to a low boil. Reduce the heat to low, cover, and cook for 20–40 minutes, or until the barley is mushy and the water has been absorbed.

5. Remove the pilaf from the heat and set aside for 10 minutes.

6. Toss the pilaf with the parsley, chives, lemon juice, salt, and pepper, and gently fluff with a fork to mix.

7. Serve.

Garnish with mint leaves before serving.

12 teaspoon dried thyme may be used for fresh thyme in this recipe.

Per Serving Nutritional Values:

860 calories | 11.1 g fat | 39 mg sodium | 8 g carbs | 35.2 g fiber | 2.6 g sugar | 22.3 g protein

Tomato Lentil Bowl
Time to Prepare: 10 minutes

30 Cooking time

6 servings ingredients

- 2 chopped onions
- 1 tablespoon olive oil
- 2 cups washed dry brown lentils
- 4 garlic cloves
- 12 teaspoon crushed ginger
- 1 teaspoon salt
- 14 teaspoon pepper
- 12 teaspoon paprika
- 14 cup lemon juice
- 3 cups water
- 34 cup fat-free plain Greek yogurt
- 3 tablespoons tomato paste
- Optional: fresh cilantro, minced
- Tomatoes, chopped

Preparation:

1. In a saucepan, heat the oil over medium to high heat.

2. Cook the onions for 2 minutes in a skillet. Cook for a minute after adding the garlic.

3. Bring to a boil with the spices, water, and lentils. Turn down the heat.

4. Simmer for 25 minutes with the lid on the pot. Combine the tomato paste and lemon juice in a mixing bowl. Bring to a boil.

5. Serve.

Serve with yogurt, cilantro, and tomatoes as a side dish.

Substitute soy yogurt for Greek yogurt as a variation.

Per Serving Nutritional Values:

294 calories | 3 g fat | 219 mg sodium | 49 g carbs | 8 g fiber | 5 g sugar | 21 g protein

Chickpeas with Garlic and Parsley
Time to prepare: 10 minutes

Time to cook: 20 minutes

6 servings ingredients

- 1/4 cup extra-virgin extra-

- 4 finely sliced garlic cloves

- a quarter teaspoon of red pepper flakes

- 1 chopped onion

- Season with salt and pepper to taste.

- 2 rinsed 15-ounce cans chickpeas

- 1 quart chicken stock

- 2 teaspoons minced fresh parsley

- lemon juice, 2 tablespoons

Preparation:

1. In a pan, heat three tablespoons of oil and sauté the garlic and pepper flakes for three minutes over medium heat.

2. Cook for 5–7 minutes after adding the onion and 14 teaspoon of salt.

3. Stir in the chickpeas and broth, then reduce to a low heat.

4. Reduce the heat to low and cook, covered, for 7 minutes.

5. Remove the lid and increase the heat to high; cook for 3 minutes, or until the liquid has evaporated completely.

6. Toss in the lemon juice and parsley and set aside.

7. Season to taste with salt and pepper and serve.

Drizzle with a tablespoon of olive oil before serving.

If needed, season with extra salt and pepper.

Per Serving Nutritional Values:

611 calories | 17.6 g fat | 163 mg sodium | 89.5 g carbs | 25.2 g fiber | 16.1 g sugar | 28.7 g protein

Mediterranean Tomato Rice

Time to Prepare: 20 minutes

Time to Cook 20 minutes

4 servings Ingredients:

- 2 minced garlic cloves
- 1 cup chopped onions
- 2 tablespoons extra virgin olive oil
- 1 teaspoon thyme, dry
- 1 cup chopped green bell pepper
- 1 tablespoon paste de tomate
- 3 cups boiled rice
- 1 cup finely sliced celery
- 1/2 teaspoon marjoram (dry)
- 1 (15-ounce) tomato can, drained and liquid set aside
- To taste, season with salt and black pepper.

Preparation:

1. Heat the olive oil, onions, and garlic in a large pan over medium heat for approximately 5 minutes, stirring regularly.

2. Cook for another 2 minutes after adding the marjoram, celery, and thyme.

3. Cook for 3 minutes longer, stirring regularly, after adding the bell pepper.

4. Add the drained tomatoes, tomato paste, salt, and black pepper and stir to combine.

5. Fold in the rice and stir firmly to combine.

6. Remove the dish from the oven and serve immediately.

Serve with a Mediterranean vegetable curry as a side dish.

Seasonings of your choosing may be added as a variation.

Per Serving Nutritional Values:

617 calories | 8.3 grams of fat | 1.3 grams of saturated fat | 122.3 grams of carbohydrates | 4.8 grams of fiber | 6.5 grams of sugar|11.9 grams of protein

Grilled Lemon Salmon

15-minute prep time

Time to cook: 12 minutes

4 servings Ingredients:

- 12 cup plain Greek yogurt
- 3 chopped garlic cloves
- 2 teaspoons minced fresh dill
- 1 tablespoon extra-virgin olive oil
- 1.1/2 tablespoons cumin powder
- 4 skinless salmon fillets (6 oz.)
- 2 tblsp basil leaves (fresh)
- 2 tblsp. freshly squeezed lemon juice
- 1.1/2 tablespoons cilantro powder
- To taste, season with salt and black pepper.
- Cooking spray with olive oil

Preparation:

1. In a large mixing bowl, combine all of the ingredients except the salmon and basil.

2. Transfer half of the mixture to a separate bowl and refrigerate it.

3. Toss the salmon fillets in the remaining yogurt mixture in a large mixing basin and coat well.

4. Refrigerate for 30 minutes, flipping halfway through.

5. Lightly coat a baking sheet with cooking spray and preheat the broiler to medium-high heat.

6. Take the salmon fillets out of the dish and toss away any extra yogurt mixture.

7. Arrange the salmon fillets on the baking sheet and cook for 6 minutes on each side.

8. Remove the broiler pan from the oven and transfer to serving plates.

9. Garnish with basil and a dollop of the remaining yogurt mixture on top.

Serve with roasted vegetables as a side dish. Use parsley leaves instead of basil leaves as a variation. Per Serving Nutritional Values:

284 calories | 14.3 grams of fat | 2.1 grams of saturated fat | 3 grams of carbohydrates | 0.4 grams of fiber | 1 gram of sugar | 36.7 grams of protein

Salmon with White Sauce

Time to Prepare: 10 minutes

Time to cook: 25 minutes

7   servings ingredients

- 3 pounds salmon fillets
- 3 bay leaves
- 3 tablespoons flour
- 3 tablespoons almond butter:
- 1 teaspoon powdered black pepper
- 1 tablespoon olive oil
- 1 teaspoon oregano
- 1 white onion, diced
- 1 cup milk
- 3 garlic cloves, smashed
- 1 tablespoon pistachio, crushed
- 1 teaspoon salt

Preparation:

1. Season the salmon fillets with salt, black pepper, and oregano, and let them marinade for a while.

2. Meanwhile, in a saucepan, bring the milk to a boil.

3. Stir in the chopped onion and cook for 5 minutes.

4. Simmer for 4 minutes on low heat with the garlic cloves and bay leaf.

5. Remove the bay leaf from the milk, add the flour, and blend the mixture until smooth.

6. Stir in the butter and allow it to cook up in the sauce. Stir the sauce occasionally to ensure that it is properly mixed.

7. In a pan, pour the olive oil and add the marinated fish. (Depending on the size of your pan and the size of the fillets, you may need to cook in batches.)

8. On high heat, sear the fillets for 2 minutes on each sides.

9. Toss the white sauce with the crumbled pistachios.

10. Transfer the roasted salmon to a baking dish with a sprinkle of white sauce and place it in the oven.

11. Bake the fish for 15 minutes at 360°F in a preheated oven.

12. Drizzle the leftover white sauce over the salmon after it's finished cooking.

Serve with chopped parsley as a garnish.

Substitute trout for salmon as a variation.

Per Serving Nutritional Values:

359 calories | 18.9 g fat | 440 mg sodium | 8.1 g carbs | 1.4 g fiber | 2.6 g sugar | 41.1 g protein

Greek Tilapia

Time to Prepare: 10 minutes

Time to cook: 18 minutes

4 servings Ingredients:

- 4 fillets of tilapia
- 12 cup crumbled Feta cheese
- 2 tablespoons extra virgin olive oil
- 4 diced tomatoes
- 1/2 cup chopped parsley
- 1 tablespoon minced garlic
- Pepper
- Salt

Preparation:

1. Preheat the oven to 400 degrees Fahrenheit.
2. Arrange the fish fillets in a baking tray.
3. Drizzle with olive oil and season with salt and pepper.
4. Top the fish fillets with cheese, garlic, and tomatoes.
5. Bake for 15 to 18 minutes at 350°F.

Serve with a parsley garnish as a finishing touch.

Alternative: Instead of Feta cheese, crumbled goat cheese may be used.

Per Serving Nutritional Values:

231 calories | 12.3 g fat | 299 mg sodium | 6.7 g carbs | 1.8 g fiber | 4.1 g sugar | 25.1 g protein

Zesty Garlic Salmon

Time to prepare: 10 minutes

Time to Cook: 18 minutes

6 servings ingredients:

- 2 pound fillet of salmon
- 2 tablespoons chopped parsley for garnish
- Add a good proportion of Olive oil
- to taste add kosher salt
- 1/2 lemon slices to serve as a garnish

Sauce with lemon and garlic

- one lemon's zest
- 3 tablespoons extra virgin olive oil
- lemon juice (three tablespoons)
- 5 garlic cloves, peeled and cut
- 1 teaspoon paprika (sweet)
- 1/2 teaspoon oregano, dried
- 1/2 tsp. black pepper

Preparation:

1. Preheat the oven to 375 degrees Fahrenheit.

2. In a mixing bowl, whisk together the olive oil, pepper, garlic, lemon zest and juice, oregano, and paprika. It's time to make the lemon-garlic sauce!

3. Brush a baking pan with oil after lining it with foil.

4. Place the fish on the baking pan and season it with salt. Over the fish, pour the lemon-garlic sauce.

5. Bake for 20 minutes in a preheated oven.

6. Remove the roasted salmon from the oven and broil for 3 minutes before serving.

Serving Suggestion: Garnish with fresh parsley and lemon slices before serving.

Variation Tip: You may use any other dipping sauce in place of the olive oil in the lemon-garlic sauce.

Per Serving Nutritional Values:

338 calories | 25.8 g fat | 341 mg sodium | 11.8 g carbs | 3 g fiber | 2.9 g sugar | 33.1 g protein

Clams Toscano

Time to Prepare: 10 minutes

15 minutes to   cook

6 servings ingredients:

Scrubbed 36 clams in the shell

- 3 tablespoons extra virgin olive oil

- 5 garlic cloves, minced

- 1 tablespoon dried oregano

- 2 cups fish broth

- 1 tablespoon parsley, dry

- 1 teaspoon red pepper flakes, crushed (optional)

Preparation:

1. Fry the garlic for a minute in olive oil, then add the pepper flakes, broth, parsley, and oregano.

2. Toss in the clams and whisk everything together.

3. Cover the pan with a cover and heat until the clams open up.

4. Divide the mixture evenly among serving dishes.

5. Enjoy.

Garnish with cilantro before serving.

Substitute chicken stock for fish stock as a variation.

Per Serving Nutritional Values:

227 calories | 15.7 g fat | 126 mg sodium | 4.4 g carbs | 0.5 g fiber | 0.3 g sugar | 3.2 g protein

Easy Shrimp Skewers

Time to Prepare: 10 minutes

Time to cook: 10 minutes

6 servings Ingredients:

- 12 pound deveined shrimp
- 1 teaspoon paprika (sweet)
- 2 tablespoons lemon juice
- 2 teaspoon paste de garlic
- 14 cup extra virgin olive oil
- 12 tablespoon oregano, dried
- Pepper
- Salt

Preparation:

1. Toss the shrimp with the remaining ingredients in a large mixing bowl.

2. Refrigerate for 2 hours after covering with plastic wrap.

3. Thread marinated shrimp onto wooden skewers that have been soaked.

4. Cook the shrimp for 5-7 minutes on the grill. Halfway through, turn around.

Serve immediately with a garnish of chopped parsley.

Add a quarter teaspoon of smoked paprika for a more smoky taste.

Per Serving Nutritional Values:

214 calories | 10.5 g fat | 307 mg sodium | 2.8 g carbs | 0.4 g fiber | 0.4 g sugar | 26.1 g protein

Healthy Shrimp Egg Salad

Time to Prepare: 10 minutes

Time to cook: 10 minutes 4 people

Ingredients:

- 1 pound medium shrimp, peeled, deveined, and cooked
- 2 hard-boiled eggs,
- diced a quarter-cup of mayonnaise
- 1/2 chopped green bell pepper
- 2 diced celery stalks
- 1/2 onion
- 2 tbsp lime juice, freshly squeezed
- 2 radishes, diced
- 1 jalapeno pepper, chopped
- Salt

Directions:

1. In a large mixing bowl, combine the shrimp and the other ingredients.

Serve with a parsley garnish as a finishing touch.

Add your favorite salad dressing as a variation.

Per Serving Nutritional Values:

215 calories | 8.5 g fat | 440 mg sodium | 8.5 g carbs | 0.9 g
fiber | 3.1 g sugar | 27.7 g protein

Herb-Crusted Halibut

Time to prepare: 10 minutes

15 minutes for cooking

4 servings Ingredients:

- 1/3 cup parsley (fresh)
- 1/4 cup fresh chives
- 1/4 cup fresh dill
- 1 teaspoon zest of lemon
- One third of a cup of panko breadcrumbs
- 14 teaspoon freshly cracked black pepper
- 1 tablespoon olive oil
- one teaspoon of salt
- Halibut fillets, 4–6 ounces

Preparation:

1. Finely chop the dill, chives, and parsley.

2. Prepare a baking pan by lining it with foil. Preheat the oven to 400 degrees Fahrenheit.

3. In a mixing bowl, combine the salt, pepper, lemon zest, olive oil, chives, dill, parsley, and breadcrumbs.

4. Thoroughly rinse the halibut. Before baking, dry it with paper towels. Arrange the fish in a single layer on the baking sheet.

5. Crumble the bread crumbs on top of the fish and press them into the fillets.

6. Bake for 10–15 minutes, or until the top is golden and flaky.

Serve with flavorful potatoes and peas as a side dish. Use additional fresh herbs of your choice as a variation. Per Serving Nutritional Values:

273 calories | 7 g fat | 593 mg sodium | 5.1 g carbs | 1.1 g fiber | 0.2 g sugar | 38 g protein

Halibut with Kale

Time to Prepare: 10 minutes

15 minutes for cooking

4 servings ingredients:

- 3 tablespoons olive oil, divided
- 3 cups finely chopped kale
- 2 cups split cherry tomatoes
- 4 (4-ounce) boneless, skinless halibut fillets
- 1 lemon's juice and zest
- 1 tablespoon chopped fresh basil
- sea salt and black pepper to taste

Preparation:

1. Preheat the oven to 375 degrees Fahrenheit.

2. Use two tablespoons of olive oil to lightly coat an 8-inch × 8-inch baking dish.

3. Toss the greens with the cherry tomatoes and halibut in the bottom of the baking dish.

4. Drizzle the remaining olive oil, lemon juice, lemon zest, basil, salt, and pepper over the top.

5. Bake until the fish is flaky and the greens are wilted, approximately 15 minutes (about 15 minutes).

6. Finally, serve and enjoy.

Garnish with cilantro before serving.

To make serving easier, prepare the fish and veggies in individual foil packets on a baking sheet rather than in a baking dish.

Per Serving Nutritional Values:

228 calories | 10 g fat | 284 mg sodium | 9 g carbs | 2 g fiber | 2 g sugar | 28 g protein

Zesty Scallops

Time to Prepare: 10 minutes

Time to Cook 5 minutes

4 servings Ingredients:

- Scallops (1 pound)
- to taste with sea salt and black pepper
- 2 tablespoons extra virgin olive oil
- 1 lime juice pinch
- red pepper flakes
- 1 tablespoon chopped fresh cilantro

Preparation:

1. Lightly season the scallops with salt and pepper.

2. Heat the olive oil in a large pan over medium-high heat.

3. Arrange the scallops in the pan, ensuring sure they don't overlap.

4. Sear on both sides for approximately 3 minutes total, rotating once.

5. Toss the scallops in the lime juice with the red pepper flakes in the pan.

6. Serve.

Serve with fresh cilantro on top as a garnish.

Variation Tip: Look for dried scallops that aren't preserved in sodium triphosphate, a milky liquid. This ingredient causes the scallops to absorb water, resulting in a loss of taste.

Per Serving Nutritional Values:

160 calories | 8 g fat | 241 mg sodium | 3 g carbs | 0.1 g fiber | 0.2 g sugar | 19 g protein

Baked Trout With Dill

Time to Prepare: 10 minutes

Time to cook: 20 minutes

4 servings Ingredients:

- 2 (8-ounce) entire fish, cleaned
- 3 tablespoons olive oil,
- split Sea salt and black pepper to taste
- 1 lemon, cut thinly into 6 slices
- 1 tablespoon coarsely chopped fresh dill
- 1 tablespoon chopped fresh parsley
- 12 cup fish stock with minimal sodium

Preparation:

1. Preheat the oven to 400 degrees Fahrenheit.

2. Use one teaspoon of olive oil to lightly coat a 9-inch x 13-inch baking dish.

3. Rinse the trout and wipe dry with paper towels before applying the remaining two tablespoons of olive oil to the fish. Salt & pepper to taste.

4. Stuff the trout's interior with lemon slices, dill, and parsley before placing it in the baking dish.

5. Bake the fish for 10 minutes before adding the fish stock.

6. Bake for another 10 minutes, or until the salmon flakes readily with a fork.

7. Serve.

Garnish with fresh dill and lemon slices before serving.

Substitute chicken stock for fish stock as a variation.

Per Serving Nutritional Values:

194 calories | 10 g fat | 128 mg sodium | 1 g carbs | 0 g fiber | 0 g sugar | 25 g protein Time to Prepare: 10 minutes Time to prepare: 20 minutes 4 servings Ingredients:

Greek Stuffed Squid

Time to Prepare: 10 minutes

Allow 1 hour 15 minutes to cook

4 servings Ingredients:

- a quarter cup of golden raisins
- 1/4 cup roasted pine nuts
- 1/2 oz. red wine
- 1/2 cup dried baked breadcrumbs
- 1 tomato sauce can (15 oz.)
- 1 minced garlic clove
- 1 tablespoon mint (dried)
- 16 medium squid bodies, plus 6 ounces cut tentacles
- 2 tbsp extra-virgin extra-virgin olive oil
- 3 coarsely chopped onions
- 4 rinsed and minced anchovy fillets
- 5 tablespoons minced fresh parsley
- Season with salt and pepper to taste.

Preparation:

1. In a 12-inch nonstick frying pan, heat 1 tablespoon of oil over moderate to high heat until it begins to shimmer.

2. Cook until the onions are soft, about two-thirds of the way through (approximately 5 minutes). Cook for 1–2 minutes, or until the squid tentacles are no longer transparent.

3. Add the pine nuts, mint, and 14 tsp pepper and simmer for 1 minute, or until fragrant.

4. Combine the breadcrumbs, 14 cup parsley, raisins, and anchovies in a large mixing dish.

5. Season to taste with salt and pepper and set aside to cool somewhat.

6. Spoon 2 teaspoons of filling into each squid body with a small soup spoon, pushing down on the contents.

gently, leaving a 1-inch gap at the top.

7. Securely shut each squid by threading a toothpick through the aperture.

8. In the now-empty frying pan, heat the remaining 1 tablespoon of oil over moderate to high heat until it begins to shimmer.

9. Add the remaining onions and continue to sauté until they are soft (approximately 5 minutes).

10. Add the garlic, 14 teaspoon salt, and 14 teaspoon pepper and simmer for about half a minute, or until fragrant.

11. Add the wine, tomato sauce, salt, and pepper to the pan and heat to a low simmer.

12. Pour the sauce over the squid.

13. Reduce the heat to low, cover, and cook for 1 hour, or until the sauce has thickened slightly and the squid is easily punctured with a paring knife.

14. Season the sauce to taste with salt and pepper.

15. Remove the toothpicks from the squid and add the remaining 1 tablespoon of parsley to the top.

16. Serve.

Garnish with basil leaves before serving.

Add chili for a boost of flavor.

Per Serving Nutritional Values:

733 calories | 22.3 g fat | 1012 mg sodium | 44.9 g carbs | 4.9 g fiber | 14.8 g sugar | 55 g protein

Classic Calamari Stew

Time to Prepare: 10 minutes

Time to cook: 45 minutes

6 servings ingredients

- 1/4 cup extra-virgin olive oil, plus a little more to serve
- a quarter teaspoon of red pepper flakes
- 1/2 cup red wine
- 1/3 cup pitted brine-cured green olives, roughly chopped
- 2 pounds small squid, bodies sliced crosswise into
- 1-inch-thick rings, tentacles halved
- 3 (28-ounce) cans whole peeled tomatoes, drained and coarsely chopped
- 1 tablespoon capers, rinsed
- 2 celery ribs, thinly sliced
- 2 onions, finely chopped
- 2 pounds small squid, bodies sliced crosswise into
- 1-inch-thick rings, tentacles halved
- garlic cloves, minced
- 3 tablespoons fresh parsley
- Season with salt and pepper to taste.

Preparation:

1. In a Dutch oven, heat the oil over medium to high heat until it begins to shimmer.

2. Add the onions and celery and simmer until the onions and celery are soft (approximately 5 minutes).

3. Add the garlic and pepper flakes and sauté for about half a minute, or until fragrant.

4. Add the wine and simmer until almost all of it has evaporated (approximately 1 minute).

5. Using paper towels, pat the squid dry and season with salt and pepper. Add the squid to the saucepan and stir to combine.

6. Reduce the heat to low, cover, and cook until the squid has released all of its liquid (about 15 minutes).

7. Add the tomatoes, olives, and capers, cover, and simmer until the squid is very soft (about 30 minutes).

8. Remove the pan from the heat, stir in the parsley, and season to taste with salt and pepper.

Serving Suggestion: Drizzle additional oil over individual servings before serving.

Variation Tip: For a spicier taste, add chili.

Per Serving Nutritional Values:

480 calories | 13.3 g fat | 217 mg sodium | 32 g carbs | 3.8 g fiber | 1.9 g sugar | 26.7 g protein

Octopus Braised in Red Wine

Time to Prepare: 10 minutes

Time to cook:2 hours

4 servings Ingredients:

- 1 (4-pound) rinsed octopus

- 1 cup red wine, dry

- 1 rosemary sprig, fresh

- 1 tbsp extra-virgin extra-virgin olive oil

- 2 tablespoons red wine vinegar

- 2 bay leaves 2 tbsp tomato puree

- 2 tblsp gelatin (unflavored)

- 4 garlic cloves, peeled and crushed

- 2 tablespoons fresh parsley

- To taste, season with salt and black pepper. a pinch of cinnamon powder

- a pinch of nutmeg (ground)

Preparation:

1. Separate the octopus mantle (big sac) and body (lower portion with tentacles) from the head (middle section with eyes) using a sharp knife; discard the head.

2. Place the octopus in a large saucepan with 2 inches of water and bring to a boil over high heat.

3. Reduce the fire to low, cover, and cook until the skin between the tentacle joints breaks easily when pushed (45 minutes to 114 hours).

4. Transfer the octopus to a cutting board to cool somewhat.

5. Measure out 3 cups of the octopus cooking liquid and set aside; discard the rest and wipe the pot dry with paper towels.

6. Cut the mantle into quarters with a paring knife while the octopus is still warm, trimming and scraping away skin and interior fibers. Place it in a mixing dish. Remove the skin from the body with your fingers, being careful not to remove the suction cups from the tentacles. Cut the tentacles in three sections around the body's core and discard the core.

7. Cut the tentacles into 2-inch lengths and place them in a bowl.

8. In the now-empty pot, heat the oil over moderate to high heat until it begins to shimmer.

9. Add the tomato paste and cook, stirring constantly, for about 1 minute, or until it begins to darken.

10. Add the garlic, rosemary sprig, bay leaves, 12 teaspoon pepper, cinnamon, and nutmeg, and cook for about half a minute, or until fragrant.

11. Add the octopus that was set aside. Scrape up any browned bits with the cooking liquid, wine, vinegar, and gelatin. Bring to a boil, then reduce to a low heat and simmer for 20 minutes, stirring occasionally.

12. Add the octopus and any fluids that have gathered and bring to a boil.

13. Cook, tossing occasionally, until the octopus is tender and the sauce has slightly thickened and coats the back of a spoon (20 minutes to half an hour)

14. Remove the rosemary sprig and bay leaves from the pan and set aside.

15. Serve.

Mix in the parsley and season with salt and pepper to taste. Add a spoonful of paprika to make the meal more vivid. Per Serving Nutritional Values:

457 calories | 7.9 g fat | 22 mg sodium | 5.2 g carbs | 0.8 g fiber | 1.5 g sugar | 75 g protein

Octopus in Honey Sauce

Time to Prepare: 20 minutes

1 hour and 25 minutes to cook

8 servings Ingredients:

- one bay leaf
- 1/3 cup water,
- 2.1/4 pounds fresh octopus
- 2 finely chopped onions
- 1 finely sliced garlic clove
- 1 can chopped low-sodium tomatoes (14 oz.)
- a third of a cup of red wine
- 1/4 cup chopped fresh basil leaves
- 4 tablespoons extra virgin olive oil
- 1 pinch crumbled saffron thread
- 1 tablespoon paste de tomate
- 1 teaspoon of honey
- To taste, season with salt and black pepper.

Preparation:

1. Clean and prepare the octopus' head.

241

2. Cook the octopus, bay leaf, and water in a heavy-bottomed pan over medium heat for approximately 20 minutes.

3. Add the wine and cook for approximately 50 minutes, stirring occasionally.

4. To make the sauce, heat the olive oil in a pan over medium heat and cook the onions and saffron for approximately 4 minutes.

5. Cook for 2 minutes after adding the tomato paste and garlic.

6. Add the tomatoes and honey and continue to cook for another 10 minutes.

7. Pour the sauce over the octopus in the pan and simmer for approximately 15 minutes.

8. Garnish with basil and serve immediately.

Serve with egg noodles on the side as a side dish. If saffron threads aren't available, you may omit them. Per Serving Nutritional Values:

319 calories | 10.2 grams of fat | 1 gram of saturated fat | 13.9 grams of carbohydrates | 1.3 grams of fiber | 5 grams of sugar | 38.4 grams of protein

Baked Mackerel

Time to Prepare: 10 minutes

Time to cook: 20 minutes

6 servings ingredients:

- 1 teaspoon salt
- 3 tablespoons olive oil
- 1/8 teaspoon paprika
- 1/8 teaspoon black pepper
- 2 tablespoons lemon juice
- 2 pounds mackerel fillets

Preparation:

1. Preheat the oven to 350 degrees Fahrenheit.

2. In a mixing dish, combine all of the ingredients except the fillets.

3. Brush the fillets with the mixture and bake for 25 minutes in a baking dish.

Serve with baked potatoes as a side dish.

Substitute herring fillets for mackerel fillets as a variation.

Per Serving Nutritional Values:

Mahi-Mahi and Mushrooms

Time to Prepare: 10 minutes

Time to prepare: 25 minutes

4 people Ingredients:

- 3 tablespoons olive oil, split

- 1/4 cup lemon juice

- 1/4 cup fresh chives, minced

- 1/4 cup pine nuts or other nuts of your choice

- 1 big onion, diced

- 5 pounds portobello mushrooms, chopped

- Salt and black pepper to taste

- 3/4 cup bell pepper, chopped

Preparation:

1. Lightly cook the fish in olive oil in a large pan over medium heat for 8 minutes, or until it starts to flake. Turn off the heat.

2. In the remaining oil, add the bell peppers, onions, lemon juice, and mushrooms. Salt & pepper to taste. Cook until the peppers are soft, about 10 minutes.

3. Place the fish fillets on top and season with salt and black pepper.

4. Cook for a few minutes more, or until the fish is fully done.

Serving Suggestion: Before serving, garnish with toasted pine nuts and chives.

Salmon may be used instead of mahi-mahi as a variation.

Per Serving Nutritional Values:

444 calories | 16.6 g fat | 148 mg sodium | 27 g carbs | 8.3 g fiber | 3.4 g sugar | 53.9 g protein

Citrus Scallops

Time to Prepare: 10 minutes

Time to cook: 18 minutes

4   serving ingredients

- 1 pound sea scallops

- 5 chopped green onions,

- Add Salt and black pepper to taste

- 3 tablespoons olive oil

- 1/4 teaspoon red pepper flakes

- 4 medium oranges, peeled and sectioned

- 2 teaspoons fresh cilantro or parsley, diced

- 3 tablespoons lime juice

- 4 garlic cloves, minced

Preparation:

1. Lightly fry the onions, garlic, and pepper in olive oil in a large skillet until the vegetables are soft.

2. Add the scallops and season with salt, pepper, and black pepper. Cook the scallops until they are fully cooked. Pour in the lime juice.

3. Remove the pan from the heat and add the orange slices and fresh cilantro.

4. Cook thescallops until they are lightly golden brown.

5. Turn off the heat and serve.

Garnish with parsley before serving.

Change it up with clementine or grapefruit instead of oranges.

Per Serving Nutritional Values:

275 calories | 11.7 g fat | 187 mg sodium | 23.7 g carbs | 4.2 g fiber | 14.4 g sugar | 21.1 g protein

Cheesy Tilapia
Time to Prepare: 10 minutes

15 minutes to cook

7 servings ingredients:

- 1/4 cup of flour

- 1 tablespoon olive oil

- 2 pounds tilapia fillet

- 1 teaspoon dried dill

- 7 oz. grated parmesan cheese

- paprika (1 tablespoon)

- 1 teaspoon oregano, dried

Preparation:

1. Combine the paprika, dried dill, dry oregano, and flour. Mix well.

2. Pour the olive oil into a pan and heat over medium heat.

3. Rub the oregano mixture into the tilapia fillets.

4. In a skillet, sear the tilapia for 10 minutes on both sides.

5. Sprinkle the grated cheese over the fish and cover it with a lid.

6. Cook the tilapia for 2 minutes longer.

7. Serve hot!

Serving Suggestion: Serve with your favorite greens.

Add a pinch of chile for a spicier flavor.

Per Serving Nutritional Values:

235 calories | 9.4 g fat | 310 mg sodium | 5.2 g carbs | 0.6 g fiber | 0.1 g sugar | 33.9 g protein

Grilled Salmon

Time to Prepare: 10 minutes

Time to cook: 27 minutes

6 servings ingredients

- Salmon fillet weighing 1.1/2 pounds
- 1 tablespoon powdered garlic
- One third of a cup of soy sauce
- One third of a cup of brown sugar
- water (1/3 cup)
- 1/4 cup extra virgin olive oil
- Season with salt and pepper to taste.
- 1 lemon, freshly squeezed

Preparation:

1. Rub the lemon, pepper, salt, and garlic powder into the salmon fillets.

2. In a small bowl, whisk together the soy sauce, brown sugar, water, and olive oil until the sugar is dissolved.

3. Combine the fish and the soy sauce mixture in a large resealable plastic bag, lock, and marinate for at least 2 hours.

4. Preheat the oven to 350°F and preheat the broiler. A griddle pan should be lightly oiled.

5. Remove the salmon from the marinade and place it in the pan.

6. Broil the salmon for 7 minutes on each side, or until it flakes easily when tested with a fork.

Serve with some greens as a side dish.

Add a pinch of chile for more spiciness.

Per Serving Nutritional Values:

318 calories | 20.1 g fat | 987 mg sodium | 13.2 g carbs | 3 g fiber | 1.9 g sugar | 20.5 g protein

Meat Recipes

Lamb Chops with Veggies

Time to Prepare: 20 minutes (plus 3 hours for marinating)

Time to Cook: 27 minutes

4 servings Ingredients:

- 1/2 cup basil leaves, fresh

- lamb loin chops, 8 (4 oz.)

- 1/2 cup mint leaves, fresh

- 2 cloves garlic

- 2 sliced zucchinis

- 1 sliced eggplant

- ounces cherry tomatoes, fresh

- 1 tablespoon rosemary leaves, fresh

- 3 tablespoons olive oil

- 1 seeded and chunked red bell pepper

- feta cheese, crumbled (1.3/4 ounces)

Preparation:

1. Preheat oven to 390°F and butter a large baking sheet gently.

2. In a food processor, puree the fresh herbs, garlic, and 2 tablespoons olive oil until smooth.

3. Place the herb mixture in a large mixing dish.

4. Toss the lamb chops in the basin with the herb mixture and coat liberally.

5. Refrigerate for 3 hours to marinate.

6. Drizzle the remaining olive oil over the zucchini, eggplant, and bell pepper on a baking sheet.

7. Arrange the lamb chops in a single layer on top of the sauce and bake for 20 minutes.

8. Remove the chops from the pan and arrange them on a serving plate. To keep the chops warm, wrap them with foil.

9. Sprinkle the feta cheese over the vegetables on the baking sheet.

10. Bake for another 7 minutes before transferring to a serving plate.

Serving Suggestion: Serve with your favorite dip.

Parsley leaves may be added as a variation.

Per Serving Nutritional Values:

619 calories | 30.6 g fat | 9.4 g saturated fat | 17.1 g carbohydrates | 7.4 g fiber | 8.7 g sugar | 69.2 g protein

Beef Kebabs

Time to prepare: 10 minutes + 12 hours of marinating

15 minutes to cook

10 people Ingredients:

1 tablespoon olive oil

• 4 pounds beef sirloin, cut into cubes

• 2 onions, quartered

• 1 big bell pepper, chopped into large pieces

• 5 small tomatoes, halved

• Season with salt and pepper to taste.

To serve

• Thick, crusty bread slices

For the marinade, combine the following ingredients.

- garlic cloves, chopped or mashed into a paste

- 4 bay leaves, crumbled

- 3/4 cup red wine of choice

- 3 tablespoons extra virgin olive oil

Preparation:

1. Combine the marinade ingredients in a shallow dish or Ziploc bag and set aside. Add the meat cubes and marinate for at least an hour.

2. Alternate skewering the steak with the onion, bell pepper, and tomato. Before using bamboo skewers, soak them in water for 1 hour.

3. Drizzle olive oil over the top and season with salt and pepper.

4. Broil or cook on a grill pan (medium heat). Cooking time is determined by the degree of doneness required (about 8 to 15 minutes).

5. Serve.

Serve with bread pieces as a side dish.

Substitute lamb for the beef in this recipe.

Per Serving Nutritional Values:

451 calories | 19.6 g fat | 370 mg sodium | 5.1 g carbs | 1.2 g fiber | 2.7 g sugar | 55.4 g protein

Pork Skewers

Time to Prepare: 10 minutes

Time to cook: 8 minutes

6 people

Ingredients:

- 2 lb. pork tenderloin, cubed into 1-inch chunks
- 1/2 cup extra virgin olive oil
- 1/2 cup white vinegar
- 1 tablespoon garlic, diced
- 3 tablespoons fresh parsley
- 1 chopped onion
- Pepper
- Salt

Preparation:

1. Combine the meat and the other ingredients in a zip-lock bag, seal it, and store it in the refrigerator overnight.

2. Thread marinated meat pieces onto wooden skewers that have been soaked.

3. Prepare the grill by preheating it.

4. Cook the meat skewers for 4 minutes on each side on the grill.

Serve with a parsley garnish as a finishing touch.

Seasonings of your choosing may be added as a variation.

Per Serving Nutritional Values:

375 calories | 22.2 g fat | 116 mg sodium | 2.5 g carbs | 0.5 g fiber | 0.9 g sugar | 39.9 g protein

Lamb Stew

Preparation time: 10 minutes

For four people, it takes 30 minutes to cook

Ingredients:

- 2 pound chunked leg of lamb
- 1 tsp oregano, dried
- 1 tbsp olive oil (extra virgin)
- 1 tablespoon garlic, minced
- 1 cup tomatoes, chopped
- 1 cup olives, pitted
- sliced a single onion
- 1/2 cup cilantro,
- chopped
- Pepper
- Salt

Directions:

1. Add the oil to the instant pot and set it to sauté mode.

2. Add the onion, garlic, and oregano and cook for 5 minutes.

3. Cook for another 5 minutes after adding the meat.

4. Gently fold in the remaining ingredients.

5. Cover and cook for 20 minutes on high.

6. Allow the pressure to naturally release after you're finished. Remove the lid.

Serving Suggestion: Garnish with cilantro before serving.

As an alternative, shredded cheese may be sprinkled on top.

514 calories per serving | 23.9 g fat | 204 mg sodium | 7.4 g carbohydrates | 2.5 g fiber | 2.4 g sugar | 64.9 g protein

Roasted Pepper Artichoke Beef

Time to Prepare: 10 minutes

Time to cook: 6 hours

- servings Ingredients:

- 2 lbs stew beef, cubed into

- 1-inch chunks

- 1/2 ounces drained and sliced roasted red peppers

- 1/2 ounces drained and sliced artichoke hearts

- 1 teaspoon basil (dried)

- 1 teaspoon oregano, dry

- 1 diced onion

- 1/2 cup sauce marinara

Directions:

1. In a slow cooker, combine all of the meat and additional ingredients and mix thoroughly.

2. Cook on low for 6 hours, covered.

Allow to cool for a few minutes before serving. Add 14 cup finely chopped parsley as a variation. Per Serving Nutritional Values:

325 calories | 11 g fat | 445 mg sodium | 19.9 g carbs | 5.9 g fiber | 9.4 g sugar | 37 g protein

Roasted Pork Tenderloin

Time to prepare: 1 hour and 10 minutes Time for cooking:

4 servings Ingredients:

- 1/4 cup extra virgin olive oil

- 1/4 cup chopped fresh rosemary

- 1 lemon's juice

- 1 lime (juice and zest)

- 1 teaspoon minced garlic

- 1 teaspoon cumin powder

- To taste season with sea salt

- Boneless pork tenderloin, 1/2 oz.

Preparation:

1. In a medium mixing bowl, combine the salt, olive oil, rosemary, lemon juice, lime juice, lime zest, garlic, and cumin.

2. Toss in the pork tenderloin in the bowl and coat well. Refrigerate for 1 hour after covering.

3. Preheat the grill to medium high.

4. Grill the tenderloin for 20 minutes, flipping it several times and basting it with the leftover marinade until cooked through (internal temperature: 140°F).

5. Take the tenderloin off the grill, cover it with foil, and set it aside for 10 minutes to rest.

6. Serve.

Garnish with cilantro sprigs before serving.

Alternatively, roast the tenderloin on a baking sheet in a 400°F oven for 25–30 minutes, or until cooked through.

Per Serving Nutritional Values:

201 calories | 15 grams of fat | 81 milligrams of sodium | 1 gram of carbohydrates | 0.1 gram of fiber | 0.2 milligrams of sugar | 20 grams of protein

Sriracha Lamb Chops
Time to Prepare: 10 minutes

Time to cook: 10 minutes

4 servings Ingredients:

- 4 loin lamb chops (4 ounces) with bones, trimmed
- to taste add sea salt and black pepper
- 1 tablespoon extra virgin olive oil
- 2 tbsp. sriracha chili sauce
- 1 tablespoon chopped fresh cilantro

Preparation:

1. Preheat the oven to 450 degrees Fahrenheit.

2. Season the lamb chops with a pinch of salt and pepper.

3. Heat the olive oil in a large ovenproof skillet over medium-high heat.

4. Brown the chops on both sides for approximately 2 minutes each, then add sriracha on top.

5. Roast the skillet in the oven until done to your liking, around 4–5 minutes for medium.

6. Serve.

Serve with a garnish of cilantro.

Use pork tenderloin or chicken instead of lamb in the same proportions.

Per Serving Nutritional Values:

223 calories | 14 g fat | 116 mg sodium | 1 g carbs | 0 g fiber | 1 g sugar | 23 g protein

Thyme Lamb

Time to Prepare: 10 minutes

Time to cook: 20 minutes

4 servings ingredients:

- Lamb shanks, 8 oz.

- 1 tblsp thyme (optional)

- 1 teaspoon minced garlic

- 1 tblsp balsamic vinaigrette

- To taste, season with salt and black pepper.

- 1 tablespoon extra virgin olive oil

- 1/2 cup of water

- 1 tablespoon chopped fresh dill

Preparation:

1. Rub the thyme, chopped garlic, balsamic vinegar, salt, and ground black pepper into the lamb shanks.

2. Drizzle olive oil over the meat and let aside for 15 minutes to marinate.

3. Add the fresh dill to the marinated lamb in an Instant Pot or pressure cooker.

4. Pour in the water and cover the pot.

5. Cook on high pressure for 20 minutes.

6. Transfer the meat to a dish after a natural pressure release.

7. Finally, serve and enjoy!

Garnish with fresh rosemary before serving. Switch out the lamb shanks with lamb shoulder as a variation. Per Serving Nutritional Values:

284 calories | 15.5 g fat | 93 mg sodium | 2.6 g carbs | 0.9 g fiber | 0.1 g sugar | 32.4 g protein

Easy Beef Roast

Time to Prepare: 10 minutes

Time to cook: 35 minutes

2 servings ingredients:

- 1.1/2 tablespoons rosemary

- 12 teaspoon minced garlic

- 2 pounds roast beef

- 1/3 cup soy sauce

- Season with salt to taste

Preparation:

1. In a mixing dish, combine the soy sauce, salt, rosemary, and garlic.

2. Place the roast in a pressure cooker or Instant Pot. Pour enough water to cover it, then pour the soy sauce mixture on top; gently whisk to combine, then cover.

3. Cook for 35 minutes on high pressure.

4. Allow for a natural release of pressure. Open the cover carefully and shred the meat.

5. Serve immediately.

Serve with a simple salad as a side dish.

Add a pinch of chile for more spiciness.

Per Serving Nutritional Values:

423 calories | 14 g fat | 884 mg sodium | 12 g carbs | 0.7 g fiber | 0.7 g sugar | 21 g protein

Baked Lamb Patties

10 minutes preparation time

15 minutes to cook

4 servings Ingredients:

- 1 teaspoon cinnamon

- 1 pound ground lamb

- 1 teaspoon coriander, chopped

- 1/4 teaspoon pepper

- 1 tablespoon chopped garlic

- 1 teaspoon cumin powder

- 1/4 cup chopped fresh parsley

- 1/4 cup minced onion

- 1/4 teaspoon cayenne

- 1/2 tblsp allspice

- 1 tsp. salt (kosher)

Directions:

1. Preheat the oven to 450 degrees Fahrenheit.

2. In a mixing dish, combine the ground beef and the additional ingredients.

3. Shape the meat mixture into patties and lay them on the baking pan.

4. Preheat oven to 350°F and bake for 12-15 minutes.

Serving Suggestion: Serve with a dip of your choice.

Seasonings of your choosing may be added as a variation.

Per Serving Nutritional Values:

223 calories | 8.5 g fat | 672 mg sodium | 2.6 g carbs | 0.8 g fiber | 0.4 g sugar | 32.3 g protein

Lamb Kofta

Time to Prepare: 20 minutes

Time to Cook 10 minutes

6 servings ingredients:

- 2 tbsp plain Greek yogurt (fat-free)
- 2 tablespoons chopped onion
- 1 pound ground lamb
- 2 tblsp cilantro, finely minced
- 1 teaspoon cumin powder
- To taste, season with salt and black pepper.
- 2 teaspoons minced garlic
- 1 teaspoon cilantro powder
- 1 teaspoon turmeric powder
- 1 tablespoon extra virgin olive oil

Preparation:

1. In a large mixing basin, combine all of the ingredients and stir thoroughly.

2. Form the ingredients into 12 oblong patties of equal size.

3. In a large nonstick skillet, heat the olive oil over medium-high heat.

4. Add the patties and cook for approximately 10 minutes, rotating regularly, until browned on both sides.

5. Plate and serve.

Serve the koftas with yogurt sauce as a side dish. Red chili powder may be used as a spice variation. Per Serving Nutritional Values:

169 calories | 8 grams of fat | 2.3 grams of saturated fat | 1.2 grams of carbohydrates | 0.2 grams of fiber | 0.3 grams of sugar | 21.9 grams of protein

Pork and Peas

Time to prepare: 10 minutes

Time tocook: 20 minutes

4 servings Ingredients:

- Snow peas, 4 oz.

- avocado oil (two teaspoons)

- 3/4 cup beef stock

- 1 pound boneless pork loin, cubed

- 1/2 cup chopped red onion

- To taste, season with salt and white pepper.

Preparation:

1. Heat the oil in a pan over medium-high heat. Brown for 5 minutes with the meat.

2. Toss in the peas and the other ingredients, bring to a boil, and cook for 15 minutes over medium heat.

3. Divide among plates and serve immediately.

Serve with mashed potatoes as a side dish. Green onions may be substituted as a variation. Per Serving Nutritional Values:

332 calories | 16.5 g fat | 219 mg sodium | 20.7 g carbs | 10.3 g fiber | 1.8 g sugar | 26.5 g protein

Garlic Veal

Time to Prepare: 10 minutes

Time to cook: 50 minutes

6 servings ingredients

- smashed garlic cloves

- 3 pounds cubed veal

- 1 cup broth

- 1 glass wine

- 3 tablespoons sour cream

- 4 tablespoons olive oil

- a handful of chives and parsley

- sea salt to taste

- ground black pepper to taste

Preparation:

1. Brown the veal cubes in olive oil for several minutes while continually stirring.

2. Add the chives and parsley and cook for a few minutes.

3. Season with salt and pepper to taste.

4. Pour in a cup of broth.

5. Continue to simmer until the meat is soft. As required, add extra broth.

6. Add the sour cream and a glass of wine when the meat is soft and cooked through, and simmer for another 5 minutes.

7. Serve.

Garnish with basil before serving.

You may use vegetable, meat, or chicken broth as a variation.

Per Serving Nutritional Values:

508 calories | 27.9 g fat | 399 mg sodium | 1.9 g carbs | 0.1 g fiber | 0.3 g sugar | 56.4 g protein

Almond-Crusted Rack of Lamb

Time to prepare: 10 minutes

Time to cook: 35 minutes

2 servings ingredients:

- 2 minced garlic cloves

- 1/2 tbsp. extra virgin olive oil

- To taste, season with salt and black pepper.

- Rack of lamb weighing 3/4 pounds

- 1 organic tiny egg

- 1 heaping spoonful of breadcrumbs

- 2 oz. finely chopped almonds

- 12 tbs rosemary, freshly crumbled

Preparation:

1. Preheat the oven to 350 degrees Fahrenheit.

2. In the meanwhile, grease a baking pan with oil and put it aside.

3. In a mixing bowl, combine the garlic, oil, salt, and freshly cracked black pepper. Coat the rack of lamb with the mixture and massage it all over.

4. Crack one egg into a bowl, mix it together until smooth, and put it away until needed.

5. In a separate dish, combine the breadcrumbs, almonds, and rosemary and whisk to combine.

6. Dredge the seasoned rack of lamb in the breadcrumbs mixture until it is equally coated on both sides, then lay it on the prepared baking pan.

7. Bake for 35 minutes in a preheated oven, or until well done.

8. Transfer the rack of lamb to a serving dish and serve immediately.

Serving Suggestion: Serve with asparagus on the side.

If desired, add chile to the mix.

Per Serving Nutritional Values:

471 calories | 31.6 g fat | 145 mg sodium | 8.5 g carbs | 3.1 g fiber | 1.5 g sugar | 39 g protein

Grilled Paprika Lamb Chops

Time to Prepare: 10 minutes

15 minutes to cook

4 servings ingredients:

- 2 racks of lamb, chopped into chops

- salt and black pepper to taste

- 3 tablespoons paprika

- a third of a cup of cumin powder

- 1 teaspoon cayenne pepper

Preparation:

1. In a mixing bowl, combine the paprika, cumin, chile, salt, and pepper.

2. Add the lamb chops and coat them in the mixture.

3. Place the lamb chops on a grill pan over medium heat and cook for 5 minutes.

4. Flip and cook for another 5 minutes; flip one more.

5. Cook for 2 minutes on one side, then turn and cook for another 2 minutes.

6. Finally, serve and enjoy.

Serve with rosemary sprigs as a garnish. If you want a milder flavor, leave off the chili powder. Per Serving Nutritional Values:

392 calories | 17 g fat | 164 mg sodium | 11.6 g carbs | 4.2 g fiber | 1 g sugar | 32.1 g protein

Parmesan Pork Chops

Time to Prepare: 10 minutes

15 minutes to cook

6 servings ingredients

- 1 tablespoon salt
- 1 teaspoon black pepper
- 1 teaspoon chili flakes
- 2 pounds pork loin
- 1 cup breadcrumbs
- 2 teaspoons Italian seasoning
- 3 tablespoons olive oil
- 5 ounces grated parmesan

Preparation:

1. Cut the pork loin into serving chops using a sharp knife. After that, season the pork chops with salt and freshly ground black pepper.

2. Stir in the chile flakes.

3. Combine the breadcrumbs and Italian seasoning in a mixing bowl and whisk with a fork. Stir in the shredded parmesan cheese.

4. Heat the olive oil in a pan over medium-high heat.

5. Carefully coat the pork chops in the breadcrumb mixture.

6. Fry the pork chops for 10 minutes on each sides in the prepared olive oil.

7. Allow the cooked pork chops to cool.

Serve with lemon wedges as an accompaniment.

Add paprika for a more flavorful variation.

Per Serving Nutritional Values:

574 calories | 34.1 grams of fat | 1608 milligrams of sodium | 14.1 grams of carbohydrates | 1 gram of fiber | 1.1 grams of sugar | 51.3 grams of protein

Herbed Lamb Cutlets

Time to prepare: 10 minutes

Time to cook: 45 minutes

6 servings ingredients:

- 2 seeded and cut into bits red bell peppers
- 1 big peeled sweet potato, cut into bits
- 2 zucchinis, peeled and cut into bits
- 1 red onion, peeled and sliced into wedges
- 1 tablespoon extra virgin olive oil
- fat-trimmed lean lamb cutlets
- 1 tablespoon chopped fresh thyme
- 2 teaspoons chopped mint leaves
- a pinch of freshly ground black pepper, to taste

Preparation:

1. Preheat the oven to 392 degrees Fahrenheit.

2. Place the bell peppers, zucchinis, sweet potatoes, and onion in a large baking dish. Season with salt and pepper after drizzling the oil over them.

3. Roast for around 25 minutes in a preheated oven.

4. Combine the herbs with a few more twists of crushed black pepper and coat the cutlets with the mixture.

5. Using a spatula, remove the vegetables from the oven and place them to one side of the casserole.

6. Roast the lamb cutlets for 10 minutes on the opposite side of the dish.

7. Flip the cutlets and simmer for another 10 minutes, or until the vegetables are cooked through (lightly charred and tender).

8. Toss everything together on the platter and eat!

Serve with roasted Brussels sprouts as an accompaniment. Variation Tip: Roast for a few minutes longer until desired doneness is reached. Per Serving Nutritional Values:

429 calories | 29 grams of fat | 320 milligrams of sodium | 23 grams of carbohydrates | 1.3 grams of fiber | 2.1 grams of sugar | 19 grams of protein

Healthy Chicken Salad

Time to Prepare: 10 minutes

Time to coook: 5 minutes

4 people Ingredients:

- 2 ounces chopped walnuts

- ounces cooked and diced chicken

- 2 teaspoons green onion

Dressing Ingredients:

- 1 teaspoon of lemon juice

- 2 teaspoons chopped fresh cilantro

- 1/8 teaspoon cayenne pepper

- One quarter-cup of mayonnaise

- curry powder (1 teaspoon)

- 1/4 tsp. black pepper

- 1/4 tsp. salt

Preparation:

1. Combine all dressing ingredients in a small dish and leave aside.

2. Toss together the chicken, walnuts, and green onion in a mixing bowl.

3. Toss the salad with the dressing.

Serving Suggestion: Combine all ingredients in a mixing bowl and serve.

You may also use chopped pecans instead of walnuts as a variation.

Per Serving Nutritional Values:

292 calories | 20 g fat | 394 mg sodium | 9.1 g carbs | 1.3 g fiber | 2.2 g sugar | 20.3 g protein

Oregano Grilled Chicken

Time to Prepare: 10 minutes

Time to cook: 20 minutes

4 servings Ingredients:

- a quarter-cup of lemon juice
- 1/2 cup extra-virgin extra-virgin olive oil
- 3 teaspoons minced garlic
- 2 teaspoons oregano (dried)
- 1 teaspoon crushed red pepper
- 1 teaspoon kosher salt
- 2 pound chicken breasts, boneless and skinless

Preparation:

1. In a medium mixing bowl, combine the garlic, lemon juice, olive oil, oregano, red pepper flakes, and salt.

2. Cut a chicken breast in half horizontally to make two thin slices. Carry on with the remainder of the chicken breasts in the same manner.

3. Place the chicken in the marinate dish and let aside for at least 10 minutes before cooking.

4. Heat some oil in a skillet over high heat.

5. Cook the breasts for 10 minutes on each side, flipping halfway through.

6. Serve immediately.

Serve with lemon wedges as an accompaniment. For a milder flavor, leave off the red pepper flakes. Per Serving Nutritional Values:

479 calories | 32 grams of fat | 943 milligrams of sodium | 5 grams of carbohydrates | 1 gram of fiber | 1 gram of sugar | 47 grams of protein

Chicken with Artichoke

Time to Prepare: 10 minutes

Time to cook: 8 hours

6 servings ingredients:

- skinless and boneless chicken thighs
- 1 teaspoon basil (dried)
- 1 teaspoon oregano, dry
- 10 ounces frozen artichoke hearts
- 14 pitted olives
- 1/4 ounces chopped tomatoes from a can
- a quarter teaspoon of garlic powder
- 3 tblsp. freshly squeezed lemon juice
- Pepper
- Salt

Directions:

1. Season the chicken with salt and pepper before placing it in the slow cooker.

2. Combine the remaining ingredients and pour over the chicken.

3. Cook on low for 8 hours, covered.

Allow time for the dish to cool fully before serving.

Add 1 tiny sliced onion as a variation.

Per Serving Nutritional Values:

329 calories | 12.1 g fat | 429 mg sodium | 9.5 g carbs | 4.2 g fiber | 3 g sugar | 44.6 g protein

Greek Roasted Pepper Chicken

Time to Prepare: 10 minutes

Time to cook: 4 hours

6 servings ingredients:

- 2 pound skinless and boneless chicken thighs
- 1/2 cup stock (chicken)
- a third of a cup of olives
- 1 tsp oregano (oregano)
- 1 cup chopped roasted red peppers
- 1 tablespoon minced garlic
- capers (1 tablespoon)
- 1 teaspoon rosemary (optional)
- 1 teaspoon thyme, dry
- 1 tablespoon extra virgin olive oil
- 1/2 cup chopped onion
- Pepper
- Salt

Directions:

1. In a large skillet, heat the oil over medium-high heat.

2. Add the chicken and heat until it is golden brown.

3. Cook for 5 minutes after adding the garlic and onion.

4. Add the other ingredients to the slow cooker with the chicken mixture.

5. Cook on low for 4 hours, covered.

Allow time for the dish to cool fully before serving.

Seasonings of your choosing may be added as a variation.

Per Serving Nutritional Values:

344 calories | 15.5 g fat | 484 mg sodium | 4.8 g carbs | 1.5 g fiber | 1.9 g sugar | 44.5 g protein

Grill Lemon Chicken

Time to Prepare: 10 minutes

Time to prepare: 12 minutes

4 servings Ingredients:

- halves of 2 pound chicken breasts
- paprika, 1 teaspoon
- 4 minced garlic cloves
- 1.1/2 teaspoon oregano, dry
- tablespoons extra virgin olive oil
- tblsp. freshly squeezed lemon juice
- tablespoons minced fresh parsley
- Pepper
- Salt

Directions:

1. Season the chicken with salt and pepper.

2. Combine the chicken and the other ingredients in a zip-top bag. Refrigerate for 1 hour after sealing the bag.

3. Prepare the grill by preheating it.

4. Cook the marinated chicken for 5-6 minutes on each side on the grill.

Allow time for the dish to cool fully before serving.

Add 1 teaspoon of Italian spices as a variation.

Per Serving Nutritional Values:

626 calories | 38.2 g fat | 242 mg sodium | 2.5 g carbs | 0.8 g fiber | 0.6 g sugar | 66.3 g protein

Grilled Harissa Chicken

Time to Prepare: 10 minutes

Time to cook 12 minutes

2 servings Ingredients:

- 1 lemon's juice
- 1.1/2 tablespoons ground coriander
- 1 red onion, sliced
- smoked paprika, 1.1/2 teaspoons
- 1 teaspoon cumin powder
- cayenne pepper, 2 tablespoons
- 3 tablespoons extra virgin olive oil
- to taste add kosher salt
- chicken thighs (boneless)
- harissa paste, 2 tblsp.

Preparation:

1. Combine the chicken, olive oil, salt, onion, garlic, coriander, cumin, cayenne, lemon juice, and harissa paste in a large mixing bowl, then toss well to coat the chicken.

2. Position the oven rack 4 inches away from the source of heat. Preheat the oven to broil. On a broiler pan, place the chicken.

3. Broil the chicken for approximately 7 minutes on each side. The temperature of the thickest section of the cooked chicken should register 165°F on a thermometer.

Serve with a salad of your choosing as a side dish. Cayenne pepper may be left out for a milder flavor. Per Serving Nutritional Values:

142.5 calories | 4.7 g fat | 102 mg sodium | 1.7 g carbs | 2.5 g fiber | 5.6 g sugar | 22.1 g protein

Chicken with Yogurt-Mint Sauce

Time to Prepare: 25 minutes

Time to prepare: 25 minutes

4 servings Ingredients:

- 1 cup plain Greek yogurt (low-fat)
- 1 finely chopped onion
- 1 tablespoon chopped fresh mint
- 1 teaspoon chopped fresh dill
- 1 teaspoon minced garlic
- 1 teaspoon cumin powder
- 1 tsp. red pepper flakes
- 4 boneless, skinless chicken breasts (3 oz.)

Preparation:

1. Whisk together the yogurt, onion, mint, dill, garlic, cumin, and red pepper flakes in a medium mixing bowl until well combined.

2. Pour 12 cup of yogurt into a small dish. Set away in the refrigerator, covered.

3. Toss the chicken in the remaining yogurt mixture and coat well.

4. Cover and marinate the chicken for 3 hours in the refrigerator.

5. Preheat the oven to 400 degrees Fahrenheit.

6. Place the chicken breasts on a baking sheet and roast for 25 minutes, or until cooked through.

7. Toss with the yogurt-mint sauce that was set out.

Garnish with rosemary sprigs before serving.

Substitute turkey breast for the chicken breast in this recipe.

Per Serving Nutritional Values:

136 calories | 7.6 g fat | 82 mg sodium | 5.7 g carbs | 1 g fiber | 3 g sugar | 26 g protein

Feta Turkey Meatballs

Time to Prepare: 10 minutes

Time to cook: 20 minutes 6 servings

Ingredients:

- 1 gently beaten egg

- 2 pound ground turkey

- 4 ounces crumbled Feta cheese

- 14 teaspoon cumin

- 1 tablespoon fresh mint, diced

- 1/2 tsp. onion powder

- 1/2 cup almond flour

- 1/4 cup chopped fresh parsley

- 1 cup chopped spinach

- 1/2 teaspoon oregano

- 1/2 teaspoon black pepper Salt

Directions:

1. Preheat the oven to 450 degrees Fahrenheit.

2. In a large mixing bowl, combine the ground turkey and the additional ingredients.

3. Roll the beef mixture into tiny balls and lay them on the baking sheet.

4. Bake for 20 minutes at 350°F.

Allow time for the dish to cool fully before serving.

Feta cheese may be replaced with crumbled goat cheese as a variation.

Per Serving Nutritional Values:

373 calories | 22.6 g fat | 417 mg sodium | 2.2 g carbs | 0.6 g fiber | 1 g sugar | 45.8 g protein

Caprese Chicken

Time to prepare: 10 minutes

Time to cook: 20 minutes

4 servings Ingredients:

- 2 sliced boneless chicken breasts
- To taste, season with salt and black pepper.
- 1 tablespoon extra virgin olive oil
- 1 tbsp extra-virgin olive oil pesto (6 oz.)
- tomatoes, diced;
- mozzarella cheese;
- if required, grated balsamic glaze
- to taste kosher salt
- As needed, fresh basil

Preparation:

1. Preheat the oven to 400 degrees Fahrenheit.

2. In a mixing dish, combine the salt, sliced chicken, and pepper. Allow 10 minutes to pass.

3. In a pan over medium heat, melt the olive oil.

4. Cook the chicken pieces for 5 minutes on each side in the melted olive oil. Turn off the heat.

5. Place the mozzarella cheese and tomatoes on top of the pesto-coated chicken.

6. Bake for 12 minutes in a preheated oven.

7. Finally, serve and enjoy.

Garnish with balsamic glaze and basil before serving. Chicken legs may be used instead of chicken breasts as a variation. Per Serving Nutritional Values:

232 calories | 15 grams of fat | 254 milligrams of sodium | 5 grams of carbohydrates | 1 gram of fiber | 5.7 milligrams of sugar | 18 grams of protein

Buttered Creamy Chicken

Time to Prepare: 10 minutes

Time to cook: 20 minutes

4 servings Ingredients:

- 1/2 cup heavy white whisky cream

- 1 teaspoon of salt

- 1/2 cup bone soup

- To taste, season with salt and black pepper.

- 4 tbsp. butter made from cashews

- 4 half-chicken breasts

Preparation:

1. Melt one tablespoon of cashew butter in a pan over medium heat.

2. Place the chicken in the cashew butter after it is heated and melted, and cook for 7 minutes on each side.

3. Transfer the chicken to a platter after it's cooked through and browned.

4. Simmer the sauce with the bone broth, heavy whipping cream, salt, and pepper in a heated pan.

5. The sauce should thicken up in approximately 5 minutes.

6. Return the chicken to the pan with the remaining cashew butter.

7. Pour the sauce over the chicken, thoroughly covering it.

8. Finally, serve and enjoy!

Serve with chopped fresh parsley as a garnish.

Change it up with any other nut butter instead of cashew butter.

Per Serving Nutritional Values:

350 calories | 25 grams of fat | 394 milligrams of sodium | 17 grams of carbohydrates | 10 grams of fiber | 2 grams of sugar | 25 grams of protein

Turkey Meatballs
Time to Prepare: 10 minutes

Time to prepare: 25 minutes

2 servings ingredients:

- 14 ounces artichoke hearts, chopped

- 1 yellow onion

- 1 pound turkey ground

- 1 teaspoon parsley (dry)

- 1 teaspoon extra virgin olive oil

- 4 tblsp. basil (chopped) Season with salt and pepper to taste.

1. Preheat the oven to 350 degrees Fahrenheit. A baking sheet should be greased.

2. Place the artichokes in a skillet with the oil and chopped onions, and cook for 5 minutes over medium heat, or until the onions are tender.

3. In a large mixing basin, combine the parsley, basil, and ground turkey with your hands. Season with salt and pepper to taste.

4. When the onion mixture has cooled, pour it into the mixing bowl and completely combine.

5. Scoop the ground turkey mixture into balls using an ice cream scooper.

6. Place the balls on the prepared baking sheet and bake until golden brown (around 17 minutes).

7. Finally, serve and enjoy.

Serve over hot rice as a side dish. Substitute turkey for chicken as a variation. Per Serving Nutritional Values:

283 calories | 12 g fat | 232 mg sodium | 30 g carbs | 12 g fiber | 4.3 g sugar | 12 g protein

Chicken Cacciatore

Time to prepare: 10 minutes

Time to prepare: 39 minutes

8 servings Ingredients:

- 2 tbsp extra-virgin extra-virgin olive oil
- 1 entire chicken, sliced into
- pieces 1 medium onion, chopped
- 3 teaspoons garlic, chopped
- 1 medium cubed carrot
- 1 medium cubed potato
- 1 medium thinly sliced red bell pepper
- 2 cups tomato sauce
- 1 quart of tomato sauce
- 1/2 cup peas (green)
- 1 teaspoon thyme, dry
- As required, season with salt and black pepper.

Preparation:

1. In a large saucepan, heat the oil over medium-high heat.
2. Pour in the oil and heat it up.

3. Cook for 2 minutes after adding the garlic and onion.

4. Stir in the chicken and simmer for another 7 minutes.

5. In a large mixing bowl, combine the carrots, red bell pepper, potato, stewed tomatoes, tomato sauce, green peas, and thyme.

6. Reduce the heat to low and continue to cook for another 30 minutes. Salt & pepper to taste.

7. Serve immediately in a serving dish.

Serve on a bed of rice or mashed potatoes as a side dish.

Variation Tip: For a hotter meal, add chili.

Per Serving Nutritional Values:

281 calories | 8 g fat | 413 mg sodium | 14 g carbs | 3.3 g fiber | 9.6 g sugar | 39 g protein

Turkey Casserole

Time to Prepare: 10 minutes

Time to cook: 40 minutes 8 people

- 9 ounces sliced mozzarella cheese
- 1 teaspoon salt
- 1 teaspoon chili flakes
- 1 cup tomato juice
- 1 teaspoon oregano
- 4 sweet potatoes, peeled and spiralized
- 1 pound chopped turkey fillet
- 4 teaspoons olive oil
- 1 tablespoon garlic, minced
- 1 cup tomatoes, sliced
- 1 cup Italian parsley, chopped
- 2 tbsp. thick cream
- 1 tablespoon butter made from almonds

Preparation:

1. Preheat the oven to 365 degrees Fahrenheit.

2. Season the turkey with salt, chili flakes, and oregano, then toss to combine.

3. In a pan, melt the butter and add the turkey. Cook the turkey for 6 minutes, constantly stirring it.

4. Grease a large square casserole dish with olive oil. Add the cooked turkey to the mix.

5. Top with a layer of sliced tomatoes.

6. Whisk together the heavy cream, minced garlic, and tomato juice in a mixing bowl.

7. Finally, flatten the spiralized sweet potato in the dish.

8. Pour the tomato juice mixture into the pan and top with chopped parsley.

9. Bake for 20 minutes in the oven.

10. Top the prepared casserole with sliced mozzarella and bake for another 10 minutes.

11. Take the dish out of the oven and set it aside to cool for a few minutes before serving.

Serve with chopped parsley as a garnish. Substitute chicken fillet for turkey fillet as a variation. Per Serving Nutritional Values:

433 calories | 11 g fat | 710 mg sodium | 23 g carbs | 30.6 g fiber | 3.8 g sugar | 17.15 g protein

Braised Chicken with Artichokes

Time to Prepare: 20 minutes

1 hour 15 minutes to cook

4 servings Ingredients:

- 4 pieces of chicken leg quarters

- 1 tablespoon extra virgin olive oil

- 1 teaspoon salt

- 1 yellow onion, diced

- 1/2 teaspoon crushed red pepper flakes

- 10 drained and halved canned artichoke hearts

- thyme sprigs, fresh

- 1 low-sodium butter bean (16-ounce) can, washed and drained

- 4 chopped garlic cloves

- 1 tablespoon freshly ground black pepper

- 4 cups chicken broth (low sodium)

- 2 cups peppers, cherry

- 4 tbsp. freshly squeezed lemon juice

Preparation:

1. Preheat the oven to 375 degrees Fahrenheit.

2. Heat the oil in a heavy, oven-proof wok over high heat and sear the chicken for approximately 5 minutes each side.

3. Arrange the chicken on a hot plate.

4. Add the garlic, onion, salt, black pepper, and red pepper flakes to the same pan and cook for 1 minute.

5. Add the broth and bring it to a boil.

6. Turn off the heat and add the cooked chicken, cherry peppers, artichoke hearts, thyme sprigs, and lemon juice to the pan.

7. Place the pan in the oven and cover it.

8. Bake for 1 hour before adding the beans. To blend, stir everything together.

9. Place the artichoke mixture on top of the chicken leg segments in the serving dishes.

10. Serve right away.

Serve with your favorite soup as a side dish.

Chicken wings may also be used as a variation.

Per Serving Nutritional Values:

611 calories | 19.8 grams of fat | 4.8 grams of saturated fat | 74.4 grams of carbohydrates | 29.3 grams of fiber | 9.1 grams of sugar | 45.8 grams of protein

Italian Baked Chicken Breast

Time to prepare: 10 minutes

Time to cook: 18 minutes

6 servings ingredients:

- 2 pound boneless breast of chicken

- Season with salt and pepper to taste.

- 1 tblsp. thyme

- 1 sliced red onion

- 1 teaspoon oregano, dry

- 1 teaspoon paprika (sweet)

- 1 tablespoon extra virgin olive oil

- 2 minced garlic cloves

- a quarter-cup of lemon juice

- To flavor, campari tomatoes

- For garnish, chop a handful of fresh parsley.

Preparation:

1. Preheat the oven to 425 degrees Fahrenheit.

2. Put the chicken pieces in a Ziploc bag and seal it. Using a meat mallet, flatten the pieces.

3. Put the chicken in a mixing dish and season it with black pepper and salt.

4. Combine the lemon juice, garlic, oil, and spices in a large mixing bowl and completely coat the chicken.

5. Arrange the onions, poultry, and tomatoes in an oiled baking tray. Wrap foil around the tray.

6. Bake for 10 minutes in a preheated oven.

7. Bake for another 8 minutes after uncovering after 10 minutes.

Serve with a sprinkle of fresh parsley on top of the cooked chicken.

Use butter instead of olive oil as a variation.

Per Serving Nutritional Values:

290 calories | 11.5 g fat | 138 mg sodium | 11 g carbs | 0.8 g fiber | 2.1 g sugar | 35.9 g protein

Turkey Cutlets

Time to Prepare: 10 minutes

Time to cook: 10 minutes

7 servings ingredients:

- 1/4 cup spinach

- 14 cup Italian parsley

- 1 tablespoon oregano

- 2 tablespoons garlic, minced

- 3 tablespoons olive oil

- 1 cup breadcrumbs

- 1 teaspoon chili flakes

- 2 pounds ground turkey

- 1 teaspoon salt

- 1 teaspoon ground black pepper

- 1 teaspoon fresh ginger

- 14 cup spinach

- 14 cup Italian parsley

- 1 tablespoon oregano

- 2 tablespoons garlic, minced

Preparation:

1. Carefully wash the spinach and Italian parsley before chopping them coarsely and blending them.

2. Combine the oregano, minced garlic, chili flakes, salt, ground black pepper, and fresh ginger in a large mixing bowl. 3 minutes of pulsing the mixture In a large mixing basin, combine the ingredients.

3. Toss in the ground turkey and stir well.

4. Shape the meat mixture into cutlets and cover each one with breadcrumbs.

5. In a pan, heat the olive oil until it shimmers.

6. Cook the cutlets for 2 minutes on each side in the preheated pan over medium heat.

7. Once all of the cutlets are done, pat them dry with a paper towel.

8. Toss the cooked item with the garlic sauce and serve.

Serve with a salad as a side dish.

If you want a milder flavor, leave off the chili flakes.

Per Serving Nutritional Values:

374 calories | 21.2 g fat | 588 mg sodium | 12.9 g carbs | 1.2 g fiber | 1.1 g sugar | 37.9 g protein

Italian Chicken Meatballs

Time to Prepare: 10 minutes

Time to cook: 32 minutes 20 meatballs per serving
Ingredients:

- 3 tomatoes, diced,

- to taste season with Kosher salt and black pepper

- 12 cup chopped fresh parsley

- 1 teaspoon oregano, dry

- 12 tsp. fresh thyme

- 14 teaspoon paprika dulce

- 12 tsp garlic cloves, minced

- 1 raw egg

- 1 red onion, finely sliced

- 1 pound ground chicken

- 2 tablespoons extra-virgin olive oil

- 14 cup shredded parmesan cheese

Preparation:

1. Preheat the oven to 375 degrees Fahrenheit.

2. Pour some extra-virgin olive oil into a saucepan and put it aside.

3. Combine the tomatoes, kosher salt, and onions in a large mixing basin.

4. Top with half of your fresh thyme and a drizzle of extra-virgin olive oil.

5. Pour the ingredients into your skillet and spread it out evenly with a spoon.

6. Combine the ground chicken, egg, parmesan cheese, a little extra-virgin olive oil, oregano, paprika, garlic, the remaining thyme, chopped parsley, and black pepper in a mixing bowl.

7. Combine the ingredients together and roll into 112-inch chicken meatballs.

8. Arrange the meatballs in the pan that has been prepared.

9. Bake for approximately 30 minutes in a preheated oven.

When the meatballs are done, they should be golden brown.

11. Take a bite and relax.

Serve with tomato sauce as a side dish. Add a sprinkle of chile for a spicy variation. Per Serving Nutritional Values:

79 calories | 4.6 g fat | 74.7 mg sodium | 4.1 g carbs | 0.4 g fiber | 1.4 g sugar | 7.8 g protein

Garlic Chicken Thighs

Time to prepare: 10 minutes + 12 hours of marinating

30 minutes to cook

4 servings Ingredients:

- chicken thighs (skinless)
- 1/4 cup extra virgin olive oil
- garlic cloves, crushed
- 1.1/2 tablespoons thyme (dried)
- bay leaves (two)
- 1/2 cup of wine (like sherry, marsala, or port)
- 1/2 cup broth chicken de poulet
- 2 teaspoons smoked paprika from Spain
- To taste, season with salt and black pepper.
- Garnish with chopped fresh parsley

Preparation:

1. Toss the chicken with the smoked paprika and set it aside to marinate overnight.

2. In a large skillet, heat the oil over medium heat. Cook for five minutes, until the chicken is browned but not cooked through.

3. Cook until the garlic is aromatic and slightly browned, about 3 minutes.

4. Season to taste with salt and pepper.

5. Stir in the other ingredients, except the parsley. Bring the water to a boil.

6. Simmer until the sauce has thickened and the chicken is cooked through (about 20 minutes).

7. Discard the bay leaves before serving.

Garnish with chopped parsley as a finishing touch. If you wish, you may even use breasts or legs as a variation. Per Serving Nutritional Values:

290 calories | 8 g fat | 368 mg sodium | 11 g carbs | 0.9 g fiber | 0.2 g sugar | 28 g protein

Mediterranean Chicken Stir Fry

Time to Prepare: 10 minutes

Time to cook: 25 minutes

4 servings Ingredients:

- 12 cup sliced pitted green olives
- 2 small diced tomatoes
- 1 onion
- 1 zucchini
- 14 teaspoon red pepper flakes
- 3 garlic cloves, minced
- 1 cup brown rice
- 2 teaspoons olive oil
- 1 teaspoon dried oregano
- 1 teaspoon dried basil
- 3 cups water
- 1 pound boneless chicken breasts, cubed
- Season with salt and pepper to taste.

Preparation:

1. Bring the water to a boil in a medium saucepan on the stove. Cook the rice according to the package directions. Turn off the heat.

2. In a skillet, heat the olive oil.

3. Cook the chicken in a light skillet until it is thoroughly done. Turn off the heat.

4. In the same skillet, add the onion. Combine the garlic, red pepper, basil, zucchini, and oregano in a large mixing bowl.

5. Season with salt and pepper after stirring until the veggies are softer.

6. Combine the cooked chicken, cooked rice, tomatoes, and olives in a mixing bowl.

Garnish with chopped green onions before serving.

Substitute chicken broth for water as a variation.

Per Serving Nutritional Values:

401 calories | 13.3 grams of fat | 248 milligrams of sodium | 44.1 grams of carbohydrates | 3.9 grams of fiber | 3.3 milligrams of sugar | 38 grams of protein

Chicken Liver Stew

Time to Prepare: 10 minutes

15 minutes to cook

5 servings Ingredients:

- 1 cup bourbon

- 1 pound washed chicken livers

- sherry, 1 cup

- to taste kosher salt

- a quarter-cup of sour cream

- 3 tablespoons extra virgin olive oil

- 1 tablespoon chopped fennel

- 1 tablespoon chopped chives

- 1 tablespoon chopped parsley

Preparation:

1. Season the livers with salt, set them on a dish, cover, and refrigerate until the following day.

2. Take the livers out of the fridge and rinse them to remove the salt.

3. In a skillet, heat the olive oil.

4. In a large mixing bowl, heat the oil and add the fennel and chives, stirring constantly. Cook for 7 minutes with the lid on the skillet.

5. Turn the heat up to high. Place the livers in the pan and cook them for a few minutes, stirring regularly.

6. Quickly pour in the brandy. With a lighted match, light it. Cover the pan with a lid and pour in the sherry.

7. Stir in 14 cup sour cream. Stir until the ingredients are well combined.

8. Bring to a boil, but do not overcook.

9. Turn off the heat. Add the remaining sour cream and mix well.

10. Serve.

Garnish with chopped parsley and serve with rice as a side dish.

Variation Tip: Feel free to experiment with other herbs.

Per Serving Nutritional Values:

307 calories | 19.1 grams of fat | 113 milligrams of sodium | 2 grams of carbohydrates | 0.1 grams of fiber | 0.1 milligrams of sugar | 23 grams of protein

Bruschetta Chicken Breasts

15-minute prep time

Time to cook: 40 minutes

4 servings Ingredients:

- 4 chicken breasts (6 oz.)
- Cooking spray with olive oil
- To taste, season with salt and black pepper.
- 1/4 cup chopped fresh basil leaves
- 1 tsp balsamic vinaigrette
- 1 teaspoon olive oil
- small tomatoes, diced
- 1 garlic clove, minced

Preparation:

1. Preheat the oven to 375 degrees Fahrenheit and coat a baking dish with olive oil cooking spray.

2. Season the chicken breasts with black pepper and salt.

3. Arrange the chicken breasts in the baking dish in a single layer.

4. Bake for approximately 40 minutes, covered in the baking dish.

5. Meanwhile, combine the tomatoes, garlic, basil, vinegar, oil, and salt in a mixing dish.

6. Combine all ingredients in a large mixing bowl and chill until ready to use.

7. Transfer the chicken breasts to serving dishes after removing them from the oven.

8. Toss with the tomato mixture and serve.

Serving Suggestion: Combine all ingredients in a large mixing bowl and serve with your favorite pasta.

Tip for Variation: You may use whatever tomato variety you like.

Per Serving Nutritional Values:

355 calories | 14 grams of fat | 3.7 grams of saturated fat | 4.7 grams of carbohydrates | 1.4 grams of fiber | 3 grams of sugar | 50.3 grams of protein

Peanut Butter Yogurt Bowl

Time to prepare: 5 minutes

4 servings Ingredients:

- 4 cups Greek yogurt, vanilla

- 1/4 cup creamy peanut butter

- 2 bananas, cut

- 1/4 cup of flaxseed meal

- nutmeg (1 teaspoon)

Preparation:

1. Divide the yogurt into four dishes and top with banana slices.

2. Add the peanut butter to the bananas after 30 to 40 seconds in the microwave.

3. Evenly sprinkle the flaxseed meal on top.

Serving Suggestion: Before serving, sprinkle with nutmeg.

Berries may be used instead of bananas as a variation.

Per Serving Nutritional Values:

370 calories | 10.6 grams of fat | 2.2 grams of saturated fat | 47.7 grams of carbohydrates | 4.7 grams of fiber | 35.8 grams of sugar | 22.7 grams of protein

Strawberry Popsicles

Time to Prepare: 10 minutes (plus 4 hours for freezing)

8 servings Ingredients:

- strawberries (2.1/2 cup)
- half a cup of almond milk

Preparation:

1. Remove the hulls from the strawberries and wash them in cool water.

2. In a food processor, puree the strawberries and almond milk until smooth.

3. Pour the mixture into stick-shaped molds and freeze for 4 hours.

Serve with low-fat yogurt as a side dish.

Any milk may be substituted for almond milk in this recipe.

Per Serving Nutritional Values:

56 calories | 4.6 grams of fat | 4 grams of saturated fat | 3.9 grams of carbohydrates | 1.2 grams of fiber | 2.5 grams of sugar | 0.7 grams of protein

Peach Sorbet

Time to prepare: 10 minutes

Time to cook: 10 minutes

4 servings Ingredients:

- 2 pound pitted and quartered peaches
- 2 quarts apple cider
- 1 stevia cup
- 2 teaspoons grated lemon zest

Preparation:

1. In a medium saucepan, boil the apple juice and the other ingredients, then simmer for 10 minutes.

2. Blend in a blender until smooth.

3. Divide the mixture among the cups and freeze for 2 hours before serving.

Serve with peach slices and mint leaves as a garnish. Variation Tip: For a tangier flavor, add a tablespoon of lemon juice. Per Serving Nutritional Values:

182 calories | 5.4 g fat | 50 mg sodium | 12 g carbs | 3.4 g fiber | 29.2 g sugar | 5.4 g protein

Cinnamon Honey Apples

Time to prepare: 10 minutes

6 people Ingredients:

- peeled, cored, and chopped apples

- a pinch of cinnamon

- 1 tiny glass of orange juice

- 1/8 tsp. nutmeg

- 1/3 cup of honey

Directions:

1. In a medium saucepan, combine the apples and additional ingredients and stir well. Cook over medium heat.

2. Cook for 10 minutes on low heat.

Serving Suggestion: Combine all ingredients in a large mixing bowl and stir thoroughly. Serve warm. Add 12 teaspoon vanilla essence as a variation. Per Serving Nutritional Values:

181 calories | 0.5 g fat | 3 mg sodium | 48.1 g carbs | 5.7 g fiber | 39.9 g sugar | 0.8 g protein

Mint Strawberry Treat

Time to Prepare: 10 minutes

Time to cook: 50 minutes

6 servings ingredients:

- Spray for cooking

- a quarter cup of stevia

- a total of 1.1/2 cup almond flour

- 1 teaspoon powdered baking soda

- 1 quart of almond milk

- 1 whisked egg

- 12 cup whipping cream

- 2 cups strawberries, sliced

- 1 tablespoon mint, chopped

- 1 teaspoon lime zest, grated

1. Preheat the oven to 350 degrees Fahrenheit.

2. In a mixing bowl, whisk together the egg and almond milk.

3. Combine the flour, baking powder, stevia, and grated zest in a mixing bowl. Mix thoroughly.

4. Stir in the whipped cream for another 10 minutes.

5. Gently fold in the mint and strawberries using a spoon.

6. Spray 6 ramekins with cooking spray and divide the strawberry mixture equally among them. Preheat oven to 350°F and bake for 30 minutes.

7. Allow to cool before serving.

Serve with sliced strawberries and mint leaves as a garnish. Variation Tip: You may use any sweetener instead of stevia. Per Serving Nutritional Values:

274 calories | 9.1 g fat | 48 mg sodium | 41 g carbs | 0.9 g fiber | 3 g sugar | 4.5 g protein

Cinnamon Honey Baby Carrots

Time to Prepare: 10 minutes

Time to cook: 20 minutes

4 people Ingredients:

- 1 pound carrots (baby)

- a pinch of cinnamon

- 1 teaspoon of honey

- 1 tablespoon extra virgin olive oil

Directions:

1. Toss carrots with honey, cinnamon, and oil in a mixing bowl.

2. Fill the air fryer basket with carrots.

3. Bake for 20 minutes at 375°F. Halfway through, turn around.

Allow time for the dish to cool fully before serving. You may also use maple syrup instead of honey as a variation. Per Serving Nutritional Values:

87 calories | 3.7 g fat | 89 mg sodium | 14.1 g carbs | 3.6 g fiber | 9.7 g sugar | 0.8 g protein

Watermelon Berry Popsicles

Time to prepare: 5 minutes

10 people Ingredients:

- 12 cup Greek yogurt
- 3.1/2 cup cubed watermelon
- 1/2 cup cut strawberries
- 1/2 teaspoon lemon juice
- 1/2 cup berries (raspberries)

Directions:

1. In a blender, combine the watermelon and additional ingredients and mix until smooth.

2. Pour the mixed mixture into the popsicle molds and set aside for 6 hours in the refrigerator.

Suggestion for Serving: Serve cold and enjoy.

You may also use lime juice instead of lemon juice as a variation.

Per Serving Nutritional Values:

28 calories | 0.3 g fat | 4 mg sodium | 5.4 g carbs | 0.7 g fiber | 4 g sugar | 1.4 g protein

Pomegranate Granita

Time to prepare: 4 hours and 10 minutes

Time to cook: 0 minutes

- 2 servings ingredients:

- 4 cups freshly squeezed pomegranate juice (no sugar added)

- 1/4 cup of honey

- 1/4 teaspoon cinnamon powder

- a pinch of salt

Preparation:

1. In a medium mixing bowl, whisk together the pomegranate juice, honey, cinnamon, and salt until thoroughly combined.

2. Pour the pomegranate mixture into a metal baking dish that measures 9 x 13 x 3 inches.

3. Freeze the mixture for at least 4 hours, scraping the top every 30 minutes or so with a fork until it resembles colored snow.

4. Freeze the granita in an airtight container for up to 2 weeks, scraping it with a fork when ready to serve.

Garnish with fresh rosemary before serving.

Variation Tip: Granita may be made with almost any juice or puréed fruit. Depending on the sweetness of the fruit you use in this recipe, adjust the honey accordingly.

Per Serving Nutritional Values:

205 calories | 0 grams of fat | 119 milligrams of sodium | 56 grams of carbohydrates | 0 grams of fiber | 54 grams of sugar | 0 grams of protein

Strawberry Crunch

Preparation time: 10 minutes

Time to cook: 55 minutes

18 servings Ingredients:

- 1 pound of white sugar

- 3 tablespoons flour (all-purpose)

- 3 cups fresh strawberries, sliced

- 3 cups rhubarb, cubed

Making the crumble

- flour, 1.1/2 quarts

- 1 cup packed brown sugar

- 1 cup nut butter (cashews)

- 1 pound oats

Preparation:

1. Preheat the oven to 375 degrees Fahrenheit (190 degrees Celsius).

2. Combine the rhubarb, 3 tablespoons flour, white sugar, and strawberries in a medium mixing bowl. Half-fill a baking dish with the batter.

3. Combine 112 cup flour, brown sugar, butter, and oats in a separate bowl until a crumbly texture is achieved.

4. Spread the mixture evenly over the fruit in the baking dish.

5. Bake for 45 minutes, or until golden and crisp.

Garnish with mint leaves before serving.

Substitute blueberries or raspberries for the strawberries in this recipe.

Nutritional Values Per Serving:

253 calories | 10.8 g fat | 178 mg sodium | 38.1 g carbs | 12 g fiber | 8 g sugar | 2.3 g protein

Berry Yogurt

Time to prepare: 5 minutes

Time to Cook: 5 minutes

4 people

Ingredients:

- 1.1/2 cup blackberries,
- 1.1/2 cup blueberries
- 1 tsp lime extract
- 1 quart of Greek yogurt
- 1 teaspoon of honey
- a quarter teaspoon of salt

Directions:

1. In a blender, combine the berries, yogurt, honey, lime juice, and salt and mix until smooth.

2. Refrigerate for 2 hours after covering.

Suggestion for Serving: Serve cold and enjoy. Add lemon juice instead of lime juice as a variation. Per Serving Nutritional Values:

111 calories | 1.5 g fat | 91 mg sodium | 20.3 g carbs | 4.2 g fiber | 14.6 g sugar | 6.3 g protein

Sweet Rice Pudding
Time to Prepare: 10 minutes

Time to cook 50 minutes

5 servings Ingredients:

- 2 quarts water

- a quarter teaspoon of salt

- 1 cup uncooked Arborio rice (sticky Italian rice)

- 1 cinnamon stick

- 1 lemon rind, cut into big pieces

- 1/4 cup almond butter (distributed)

- 4.1/4 cup full milk, plus 1/4 cup additional for egg yolks (if using)

- 3 beaten egg yolks (optional)

- Extract of vanilla (optional)

Preparation:

1. Combine the water and salt in a saucepan. Bring the water to a boil, then add the rice.

2. Reduce the heat to medium-low and continue to stir until the rice has absorbed virtually all of the liquid (about 20 minutes). To avoid burning it, don't let it entirely dry out.

3. Combine the cinnamon, lemon peel, half of the butter, and the milk in a mixing bowl. Raise the temperature to

medium-high. Bring to a boil again, stirring constantly, and then lower to a low heat.

4. Inspect the pan for any rice that has adhered to the bottom. Cooking time is 20 minutes.

5. Add the remaining butter and continue to stir for another 10 minutes until boiling. If using egg yolks (for a richer pudding), whisk them thoroughly with the additional milk in a separate dish.

6. Slowly pour this into the mixture, mixing well after each addition. Cook for a few minutes more to allow the yolks to cook and thicken the mixture. Pour in the vanilla extract (optional). Turn off the heat.

7. Remove the cinnamon stick and lemon rind and toss them out. Fill serving containers with the mixture

Serve with a dusting of cinnamon powder on top. Serve cold or at room temperature as a variation. Per Serving Nutritional Values:

392 calories | 10.5 g fat | 215 mg sodium | 43.4 g carbs | 2.9 g fiber | 11.9 g sugar | 11.5 g protein

Minty Coconut Cream

Time to Prepare: 10 minutes

Time to cook: 0 minutes

5 servings ingredients:

- 1 peeled banana
- 1.1/2 cup shredded coconut
- 2 teaspoons chopped mint
- 1.1/2 cup coconut water
- 1/2 avocado, pitted and chopped
- 2 tablespoons stevia

Preparation:

1. Pulse the coconut and banana together in a blender.

2. Pulse in the remaining ingredients until smooth.

3. Divide the mixture into glasses and serve chilled.

Garnish with mint leaves before serving.

Variation Tip: You may use any sweetener instead of stevia.

Per Serving Nutritional Values:

193 calories | 5.4 g fat | 121 mg sodium | 7.6 g carbs | 3.4 g fiber | 15.4 g sugar | 3 g protein

Almond Bites

Time to Prepare: 10 minutes

Time to cook 14 minutes

5 people servings ingredients

- 1 cup almond flour
- 1/4 cup almond milk
- 1 egg, whisked
- 2 tablespoons almond butter
- 1 tablespoon coconut flakes
- 1/2 teaspoon baking powder
- 1/2 teaspoon apple cider vinegar
- 1/2 teaspoon vanilla extract Ingredients

Preparation:

1. In a large mixing bowl, whisk together the whisked egg, almond milk, apple cider vinegar, baking powder, vanilla extract, and butter.

2. Knead the dough with the almond flour and coconut flakes. Add extra almond flour if the dough is sticky.

3. Roll the dough into medium-sized balls and lay them on an air fryer tray.

4. Gently press them with the palm of your hand. Cook the dessert for 12 minutes at 360°F with the cover down.

5. Check for doneness; if you want a crunchier crust, heat for an additional 2 minutes.

Serving Suggestion: Serve with your favorite hot beverage.

Switch out the almond flour with coconut flour as a variation.

Per Serving Nutritional Values:

118 calories | 10.6 g fat | 19 mg sodium | 3.6 g carbs | 1.6 g fiber | 1.1 g sugar | 4.1 g protein

Chia Seed Pudding

Time to Prepare: 12 hours and 5 minutes

Time to cook: 0 minutes

4 people

Ingredients:

- 1 teaspoon vanilla extract

- 1/2 cup chia seeds

- 1.1/2 cup rice milk

- 1/4 tsp. cinnamon

- 1/4 cup maple syrup (optional)

Preparation:

1. In a dish or mason jar, combine all of the following ingredients and stir thoroughly! Make sure the chia seeds don't adhere to the edges of the container.

2. Refrigerate the mixture overnight, covered.

Serve with fruit and mint leaves on the side. Before serving, you may add fruit as a variation. Per Serving Nutritional Values:

164 calories | 6.2 g fat | 37 mg sodium | 30.2 g carbs | 6.2 g fiber | 11.9 g sugar | 3.1 g protein

Cherry and Mint Sorbet

Time to Prepare: 3 hours and 10 minutes

Time to cook: 0 minutes

2 servings ingredients:

- 12 cup maple syrup

- 2 cups cherries

- 14 cup mint leaves

- 2 teaspoons lemon juice

- 14 cup water

- 14 cup coconut milk

Preparation:

1. In a blender, combine the components indicated above.

2. Blend on low for a few seconds, then increase to high until the mixture is thick and smooth.

3. Serve right away or keep for 2–3 hours in the freezer to harden up.

Garnish with mint before serving.

Switch out the cherries with strawberries as a variation.

Per Serving Nutritional Values:

426 calories | 15 grams of fat | 149 milligrams of sodium | 79 grams of carbohydrates | 1 gram of fiber | 73 grams of sugar | 2 grams of protein

Four Weeks Meal Plans

Week One

Day 1: Avocado Toast for breakfast; Cherry Tomatoes and Black Beans for lunch Snack: Tortilla Wraps with Veggies

Dessert: Mint Strawberry Treat Dinner: Herb-Crusted Halibut

Day 2: Vegetable Egg Cups for Breakfast

Stew with Black-Eyed Peas for Lunch

Snack: Pita with Lamb Filling and Yogurt Sauce Bruschetta Chicken Breasts for Dinner Minty Coconut Cream for Dessert

Day 3: Creamy Millet for Breakfast Snack: Butternut Squash Fries Lunch: Cauliflower Rice Cacciatore de Pollo de Pollo de Pollo de Pollo de Pollo de Poll Chia Seed Pudding (dessert)

Day 4: Breakfast: Florentine Eggs Baked Black-Eyed Peas for Lunch

Wraps of salmon and celery salad for a snack Dinner: Chicken Meatballs in an Italian Sauce Pomegranate Granita for dessert

Day 5: Cherry Oats Bowl for breakfast; White Beans with Tomato and Arugula for lunch Peanut Butter Balls as a snack

Halibut with Kale for Dinner

Cinnamon Honey Dessert Carrots in their early stages

Day 6: Oat and Berry Parfait for Breakfast; Sweet Red Lentils for Lunch Chickpea Spinach Patties are a tasty snack.

Almond-Crusted Rack of Lamb for Dinner Peach Sorbet for dessert

Day 7: Avocado Milkshake for Breakfast Peppers stuffed with spelt for lunch Carrot Cake Balls as a snack Turkey Meatballs for Dinner Strawberry Crunch as a dessert

Week Two

Day 1: Avocado Milkshake for Breakfast Salad with beets and walnuts for lunch Cauliflower Fritters are a tasty snack. Scallops with a kick

Peanut Butter Yogurt Bowl for Dessert

Day 2: Vegetable Egg Cups for Breakfast Soup with Zucchini and Basil for Lunch Sandwich with Grilled Veggies as a Snack Dinner: Turkey Meatballs with Feta Mint Strawberry Treat (dessert)

Day 3: Fruity Quinoa Bowl for Breakfast; Lebanese Bean Salad for Lunch Bruschetta Bruschetta Bruschetta Bruschetta Bruschetta Brusch

Lemon Grilled Salmon for Dinner Apples with Cinnamon and Honey as a Dessert

Day 4: Strawberry Smoothie Bowl for Breakfast

Snack: Avocado Caprese Wrap Lunch: Mediterranean Gnocchi Dinner: Harissa Chicken on the Grill Mint Strawberry Treat (dessert)

Day 5: Almond Chia Porridge for Breakfast Stew with Black-Eyed Peas for Lunch Zucchini Fritters are a tasty snack.

Dinner: White Sauced Salmon Strawberry Crunch as a dessert

Day 6: Breakfast Frittata with Chives

Cannellini Beans and Farro Stew for Lunch Snack: Pita with Lamb Filling and Yogurt Sauce Braised Chicken with Artichokes for Dinner Almond Bites (dessert)

Day 7: Cherry Oats Bowl for Breakfast Spicy Borlotti Beans for Lunch Crispy Chickpeas as a snack Halibut with a Herb-Crusted Crusade for Dinner Mint Strawberry Treat (dessert)

Week Three

Day 1: Lunch: Greek Avocado Salad Breakfast: Cheesy Potato Frittata Snack: Toasted Almonds (Easy)

Dessert: Sweet Rice Pudding Dinner: Greek Roasted Pepper Chicken

Day 2: Quinoa Porridge for Breakfast Greek Chicken Gyro Salad for Lunch Butternut Squash Fries are a tasty snack. Lemon Grilled Salmon for Dinner Pomegranate Granita for dessert

Day 3: Creamy Millet for Breakfast; Portuguese Salad for Lunch; Salmon and Celery Salad Wraps for Snack Dessert: Cinnamon Honey Baby Carrots Dinner: Classic Calamari Stew

Day 4: Veggies and Egg Scramble for Breakfast Salad with beets and walnuts for lunch Chickpea Spinach Patties are a tasty snack. Garlic Chicken Thighs for Dinner Almond Bites (dessert)

Day 5: Yogurt Bowl with Caramelized Figs for Breakfast Lebanese Bean Salad for Lunch

Sandwich with Chicken Caprese as a Snack

Dessert: Pomegranate Granita Dinner: Easy Beef Roast

Day 6: Avocado Milkshake for Breakfast

Salad with beets and walnuts for lunch Carrot Cake Balls as a snack Toscano Clams for Dinner Mint Strawberry Treat (dessert)

Day 7: Almond Chia Porridge for Breakfast Snack: Avocado Caprese Wrap Lunch: Ratatouille Octopus with Honey Sauce for Dinner Peach Sorbet for dessert

355

Week Four

Day 1: Tomato Omelet for Breakfast Salad with Pecan Salmon for Lunch Zucchini Fritters are a tasty snack. Dinner: Turkey Meatballs with Feta Dessert: Yogurt with Berries

Day 2: Yogurt Bowl with Caramelized Figs for Breakfast Cucumber and Tomato Salad for Lunch

Peanut Butter Balls as a snack Dinner: White Sauced Salmon Peanut Butter as a dessert Bowl of Yogurt

Day 3: Raspberry Oats for Breakfast; Zucchini and Basil Soup for Lunch Butternut Squash Fries are a tasty snack. Almond-Crusted Tilapia for Dinner Mint Strawberry Treat (dessert)

Day 4: Egg Breakfast Bowl for Breakfast Salad de Watermelon Mediterraneo (Mediterranean Watermelon Salad Zucchini Chips are a tasty snack. Squid with Greek Stuffing for Dinner Sorbet with cherries and mint

Breakfast on Day 5: Omelet Casserole Salad with Cauliflower and Farro for lunch Butternut Squash Fries are a tasty snack. Easy Shrimp Skewers for Dinner Sweet Rice Pudding (dessert)

Breakfast on Day 6: Spinach and Egg Scramble Casserole with Zucchini and Tomatoes for Lunch Snack: Toasted Almonds (Easy)

Dessert: Cinnamon Honey Baby Carrots Dinner: Roasted Pork Tenderloin

Day 7: Oats and Berries for Breakfast Lunch parfait: Greek Avocado Salad

Wraps of salmon and celery salad for a snack Scallops with a kick

Almond Bites (dessert)

The Last Words

Though no single Mediterranean diet fits everyone, it is generally high in healthy plant foods and low in animal foods, with a focus on fish and shellfish.

It's been linked to a number of health benefits, including lowering blood sugar levels, improving heart health, and improving cognitive function, among others.

The best part is that you can tailor the Mediterranean diet to your specific requirements. Start putting together great Mediterranean-inspired meals with things you like if you don't like salmon or sardines but like whole wheat pasta and olive oil.

The Mediterranean diet necessitates making long-term, sustainable dietary changes.

A diet rich in natural foods, such as plenty of vegetables, whole grains, and healthy fats, should be the goal in general.

Anyone who is unhappy with their diet should speak with a dietician. To help with satiety, they can recommend more or different foods.

Do you want to improve your ability to focus? Start your day with a cup of coffee and a lunch of 100% fruit juice, a whole-grain bagel with salmon, and 100% fruit juice. In addition to eating a well-balanced meal, experts advise doing the following:

Have a good night's rest. Maintain your hydration.

Exercise can aid in clearer thinking. Meditating allows you to unwind and clear your mind.

Author's Note

Thank you for taking your time to read my book, I love you
▢.

Appendix Measurement Conversion Chart

VOLUME EQUIVALENTS(DRY)

US STANDARD	METRIC (APPROXIMATE)
1/8 teaspoon	0.5 mL
1/4 teaspoon	1 mL
1/2 teaspoon	2 mL
3/4 teaspoon	4 mL
1 teaspoon	5 mL
1 tablespoon	15 mL
1/4 cup	59 mL
1/2 cup	118 mL
3/4 cup	177 mL
1 cup	235 mL
2 cups	475 mL
3 cups	700 mL
4 cups	1 L

VOLUME EQUIVALENTS(LIQUID)

US STANDARD	US STANDARD (OUNCES)	METRIC (APPROXIMATE)
2 tablespoons	1 fl.oz.	30 mL
1/4 cup	2 fl.oz.	60 mL
1/2 cup	4 fl.oz.	120 mL
1 cup	8 fl.oz.	240 mL
1 1/2 cup	12 fl.oz.	355 mL
2 cups or 1 pint	16 fl.oz.	475 mL
4 cups or 1 quart	32 fl.oz.	1 L
1 gallon	128 fl.oz.	4 L

TEMPERATURES EQUIVALENTS

FAHRENHEIT(F)	CELSIUS(C) (APPROXIMATE)
225 °F	107 °C
250 °F	120 °C
275 °F	135 °C
300 °F	150 °C
325 °F	160 °C
350 °F	180 °C
375 °F	190 °C
400 °F	205 °C
425 °F	220 °C
450 °F	235 °C
475 °F	245 °C
500 °F	260 °C

WEIGHT EQUIVALENTS

US STANDARD	METRIC (APPROXIMATE)
1 ounce	28 g
2 ounces	57 g
5 ounces	142 g
10 ounces	284 g
15 ounces	425 g
16 ounces (1 pound)	455 g
1.5 pounds	680 g
2 pounds	907 g

Made in the USA
Monee, IL
10 February 2023

27470264R00203